Inside Out:
What Makes the Person with Social-Cognitive Deficits Tick?

- ➤ Asperger Syndrome
- ➤ High-Functioning Autism
- ➤ Non-Verbal Learning-Disabilities (NLD)
- ➤ Pervasive Developmental Disorder - Not otherwise Specified (PDD-NOS)
- ➤ Hyperlexia

The I LAUGH Approach

Written by:
Michelle Garcia Winner,
M.A. S.L.P.-C.C.C.

Dedicated to Heidi, Robyn and

the students, families and teachers

I work with and continue to learn from.

Copyright © 2000 Michelle G. Winner, SLP

Editions published and revised: 2000, 2002, 2006.

ISBN 0-9701320-2-6

Published by: Michelle Garcia Winner, SLP
Speech Language Pathologist, M.A., C.C.C.
3550 Stevens Creek Boulevard, #200
San Jose, California 95117
(408) 557-8595
information@socialthinking.com
For more information on ordering this book or to find out
about workshops presented by Michelle, look at the web site:
www.socialthinking.com

Table of Contents

Table of Therapy Worksheets

INSIDE OUT:

WHAT MAKES THE PERSON WITH SOCIAL-COGNITIVE DEFICITS TICK?

Introduction:

Getting To This Point and Recognizing the Power of Social-Cognition

In the mid 1990s I took a job with our local high school district not having a clue as to why a high school would need a speech language pathologist. My previous work experiences had been at the Indiana Resource Center for Autism (IRCA) in the mid 80s and in medically based neuro-rehabilitation. I was now a mother of young children and was looking for a work schedule that allowed me maximum home parenting time, with minimal job responsibilities. Little did I know that I was about to launch into the most demanding job I had ever experienced. As it turned out, the high schools in which I worked had a great number of undiagnosed students with social-cognitive deficits. On my second day on the job I was asked to screen a 14-year-old girl who had been placed in Communicatively Handicapped classes all through school, but now was being considered for dismissal from speech and language services. As I screened her I noticed she was bright on her test performance but odd in her social presentation. I reviewed her school records and found that she was diagnosed with Pervasive Developmental Disorder-Not Otherwise Specified (PDD-NOS) at the age of 4 years old. It was astonishing to me that, with this early diagnosis, she had never been provided with a consistent treatment approach related to her being on the autism spectrum! When I met her she was enrolled in a Severely Emotionally Disturbed class demonstrating limited tolerance of the world around her. She was not developing skills towards independence. I was concerned both about her class placement and the psychotherapy based treatment model that was being provided to her. As I spoke about her with fellow teachers and psychologists, other students were referred to me to screen. To make a long story short, four years later we had created a team that assisted in identifying 14 high school students who fit on the high end of the autism spectrum. In those four years, with the assistance of our school psychologist, Chris De Lapp, we founded a parent support group and worked with teachers to understand the needs of these students. It took nearly two years of working with these students in social-cognitive therapy before we began to notice changes in their ability to take perspective and modify their outwardly exhibited social behaviors. Other teachers, secretaries and students also would note changes and come to report back to me. It was a project on campus that many of us were proud of.

In the process of building this project I planned to plug into the support network in the San Francisco Bay Area for individuals with Very High Functioning Autism and Asperger Syndrome. I was surprised to find that while we had some outstanding diagnosticians, few services were available even in the private sector to help folks with this disability, and there was no established network!

I wrote a proposal about our "autism project" and was accepted to give a workshop as part of my profession's state conference. In preparing for that workshop I reviewed the literature and current research as well as looked specifically at what I thought was contributing to my students' success. In my work I saw the benefits of teaching them specifically about their weaknesses and then providing relevant information and strategies to help them achieve greater success across a variety of situations. *Across my experience I have noted that a general problem in the treatment of persons on the autism spectrum is that educators tend to seek already developed treatment programs, often without understanding the social-cognitive deficits and related strategies that can help these students.*

It is my hope in writing this manual to describe a number of cognitive processes that are weak for persons with social-cognitive deficits, and explore related therapy techniques that help to facilitate social thinking and associated social skill development. I feel strongly that a student can only learn the abstract concepts that relate to social thinking if he understands them himself. These concepts include much more than simply learning about related social skills. Teaching a student to "use eye-contact" is one aspect, but teaching him WHY he uses eye-contact and what information he is supposed to be absorbing through its use is a whole different and crucial dimension worth teaching! I developed the acronym "I LAUGH" to describe a set of specific components of the larger abstract concepts of personal problem solving and communicative effectiveness. This model is an integration of the multitude of concepts that are often deficient in persons with social-cognition related diagnoses. This cognitive model is presented in Chapter 1.

Do different social-cognitive diagnoses demand vastly different treatment models?

The following diagnostic terms can be applied to persons with social-cognitive deficits:

- ❑ High Functioning Autism
- ❑ Asperger Syndrome
- ❑ Hyperlexia, PDD-NOS
- ❑ Semantic-Pragmatic Disorder
- ❑ Non-Verbal Learning Disabilities.

I am sure there are probably some terms that I have missed. *A question I often wrestle with is: Are our basic therapeutic approaches different for different diagnostic terms?* My experience working with persons representing all of the above diagnostic terms is that they all share some basic deficits in social-cognition. The extent to which they manifest these deficits appears to have a number of factors: neurology, personality and interventions applied within the environments in which they function. As educators we should always explore each student's personal strengths, weaknesses and learning style as part of our determination of how best to work with a student, but it is my firm belief that below these individual differences, students with social-cognitive deficits have some very universal traits. I explore these traits later when I introduce the "I LAUGH" acronym. Thus, in this manual, rather than speak to specific diagnostic labels when describing treatment processes, I will refer to students as simply having "social-cognitive deficits." Please understand that my use of "students" refers to persons of all ages from early elementary school all the way into adulthood.

In this manual I will describe techniques that are effective with a broad category of persons with social-cognitive deficits. This includes persons with Asperger Syndrome, High Functioning Autism, PDD-NOS, Non-Verbal Learning Disabilities, Hyperlexia, etc... However, the phrase "persons with social-cognitive deficits" is lengthy and does not easily form an acronym, thus these folks will mostly be referred to in this manual as "our students."

I believe the most effective treatment is one that combines teaching an understanding of specific aspects of social-cognitive deficits as well as how to use related strategies to help our students compensate in the real world.

Recognizing our own false assumptions....

Before approaching working with these students we need to realize that deficits in social-cognition are not the type of educational deficits about whom most educational professionals have generally received training . Our students' learning abilities and needs are unique when compared to the more neuro-typical population, or even the special education population.

Our students are adept in their ability to produce language and learn rote information rapidly. Generally by Kindergarten, they have large chunks of specific knowledge that are impressive to any adult. Children, who are verbally gifted and knowledgeable about the world, are considered "bright." With these bright children, assumptions are made that they will succeed across all levels of academics, and certainly achieve social success. After all, didn't the child do a wonderful job of telling about his knowledge to the adult listener? For children with social-cognitive deficits, their early weaknesses in the school environment (e.g., sensory overload, critical thinking tasks, changes in routine) can lead to at the very least, anxiety and rigidity; at the worst, behavioral meltdowns. Formalized testing of the child's intellectual and academic achievements is often provided given the parents concerns that something is "different" about their child. However, when these tests are administered the assumption is made that they test for a full range of intelligence (including social-cognition). The test results often demonstrate that the child is functioning in the range of normal intelligence (if not above), sadly, the next assumption often made is that the child's behaviors are the result of poor parenting.

For some children and parents, it takes many years to finally determine that all along our assumptions have been in error, and that our interventions have been faulty. To clarify information, allow me to state:

1. Children with social-cognitive deficits can demonstrate an excellent command of language and more rote or rule based learning while still having significant problems functioning in the world around them. Parents I work with often refer to their children as "bright but clueless."

2. Standardized testing does not explore the very flexible and abstract aspects of social-cognition. I am frequently asked to recommend good tests of social-pragmatics; this would be a test that explores a student's understanding and use of the social parameters of communication. I contend that once we take a process as abstract as communication and carve it into concrete pieces to assess, we have destroyed the actual process we are trying to assess! Multiple-choice questions can absolutely not assess social-cognition!

3. Parents do not environmentally create the problems associated with their children with social-cognitive deficits, any more, or less, than any parent contributes to a child's behavioral health.

4. Persons with social-cognitive deficits, from childhood into adulthood, often mystify both parents and educators. The imbalance between these students' strengths and weaknesses can be enormous. Adult thinking such as "since he can program the computer, he should be able to write his book report" is common, but not beneficial to the student. Understanding why this discrepancy exists is the first step towards helping the student.

5. Persons with social-cognitive deficits, regardless of the diagnostic label, desire successful social relationships and companionship. I have seen it written on the Internet, and heard it shared between professionals that "the difference

between persons with Non-verbal Learning Disabilities (NLD) and persons with Asperger Syndrome (AS) is that NLD folks desire friendships and AS persons do not." From my experience, virtually all of the high-level persons I work with, regardless of their diagnosis, desire social success and companionship. I believe that the extremely high rates of depression for the entire range of persons on my caseload can be explained by the unfulfillment of this desire.

A word of thanks....

Learning about the complexities of these students is always a team-based process. Nancy Dalrymple, my mentor and boss at the Indiana Resource Center for Autism (IRCA), contributed greatly to my knowledge about working with persons with autism. Nancy infinitely understood these persons' needs and helped to create educational programs that profoundly changed many individuals' lives. Nancy also had a terrific work ethic that my husband wishes I did not model after so much!

Katharina Strohmeyer, a fellow speech language pathologist and former boss, agreed to hire me to work with adults with head injuries when I explained that,"by staring into the brain of persons with autism I had to know something about how the brain functions or fails to function." Thankfully she believed me and then provided me with tools to be able to understand executive functioning. I did not know it at the time, but this chunk of knowledge would be very important later when developing programs for high-level students with social-cognitive deficits.

Donna Newberry and Christine DeLapp, from the Campbell Union High School District, hired me even though I hadn't previously worked in the schools. Both women were tremendously supportive as I began my campaign to try to meet the needs of persons with social-cognitive deficits, although none of us really knew what that meant at the time! They also assisted in "holding me down" when professionals in our community continued to mis-diagnose some of our students as being emotionally disturbed, or simply having just speech and language problems. Donna enjoyed telling fellow workers that "High Functioning Autism and Asperger Syndrome" did not exist in their district until I started working there.

My parents, Max and Pat Garcia, who always modeled for me that creativity and hard work get you what you want. I am grateful for my mother, a writer herself, who always encouraged me to take pen to paper and who helped to edit the final copy of this book.

Finally a large thanks to my husband, Wilson, and daughters, Heidi and Robyn, who have all participated in the world of autism by listening to my endless nightly stories. Their support and interest in my work has carried me through.

Chapter 1

Teaching large abstract concepts through smaller concrete pieces:

THE I LAUGH APPROACH

As I began to work with a variety of students in the high school district, it was not uncommon for them to have existing goals that stated they were to learn "personal problem solving" and to participate in "conversations." While these were reasonable concepts, I felt it was unreasonable for me to help them meet these lofty goals within one year. Where were we to begin? How do you really teach these concepts? What do these concepts mean?

What is personal problem solving?

General problem solving is not always problematic for persons high on the autism spectrum. In fact, problems that are grounded in factual information and do not require communication with other people are often *EASY* for these folks. For example, programming computers, fixing cars or any other technical job can be exceptionally easy for persons high on the spectrum to tackle. Personal-problem-solving requires a whole different bag of tricks. It is a process we go through to recognize how to make and act on good choices so that the events in our life that require us to relate to ourselves or others are successful. Sounds easy! However, personal-problem-solving is one of the most complex things we do. The first step of the process requires us to wade through vast amounts of information to be able to isolate and identify what the problem is that we need to evaluate or solve. *This requires perspective taking as well as thinking in terms of the whole picture (the gestalt).* Next, we have to consider the problem we have isolated and recognize that we have multiple choices, not all of them good, to solve it. We should choose what action path to take based on the anticipated consequences that each choice bears. *This requires scads of abstract thinking as well as a dose of perspective taking.* Once a problem-solving path is determined, it now gets more difficult because we generally have to employ our personal communication skills to negotiate solving a problem that involves another person. *This requires the ability to initiate, formulate, interpret (more perspective taking) and respond to language appropriately.* YIKES!

The problem-solving worksheet used with students to guide them through learning about the above process is called "How To Solve Problems Before They Become Problems." It was given this title after a student I was working with explained that he did not have to complete the worksheet because he did not have the problem *yet*. I explained that the funny thing about problem solving is that to be a good problem solver, you actually have to solve your potential problems before they become problems! This worksheet is on page 16 and will be referred to many times throughout this manual.

What is communicative success?

Communicative success is not simply social success. We are quick to realize that most of our students have real difficulty developing and maintaining social relationships without us recognizing the corresponding difficulties in the day-to-day communication that the classroom, job and/or home environments demand of them.

Communicative success is success with communication across a variety of environments and relationships. Again, this sounds like a relatively simple concept to educators who are blessed with a good dose of social-cognition (why else would we chose to personally relate to others as a profession?) However, achieving communicative success can be extremely taxing! A simple act of communication begins with observation (which requires eye-contact), gestalt thinking and perspective taking to understand where someone is 'coming from" perhaps prior to the person ever opening their mouth to speak. Then the abilities to initiate language, comprehend responses, abstract hidden meanings and formulate another associated message are required; all this, while monitoring the listener's tone, inflection and loudness of voice, body language, facial expression and proximity simultaneously and continuously throughout the interaction. Double YIKES! For these reasons, I no longer write goals for my students to "succeed at 5 minutes of conversation with a peer." As you can see from the above, this skill requires so many active and inter-related abilities that we can't possibly teach it as one concept. Chapter 5 will review more specifically how to help teach social thinking and related skills to build success in conversations.

How do we teach concepts such as personal-problem-solving and communicative success to high-level persons with social-cognitive deficits?

In my previous jobs I had extensive experience working both with students with autism and folks with head-injury or stroke. This gave me insight into the more typical issues of persons on the autism spectrum as well as an understanding of the complexities related to poor executive functioning. Executive functioning is the type of knowledge an executive needs to accomplish his high-level tasks. This includes tasks such as problem solving, organization, flexibility, prioritizing and knowing when to hire a secretary! Research has demonstrated that persons with solid intelligence as measured by an IQ test and with autism have deficits related to executive functioning (Rumsey, 1985; Rumsey & Hamburger, 1988; Minshew, Goldstein, Muenz & Payton, 1992; McEvoy, Rogers & Pennington, 1993). To provide for the needs of persons high on the autism spectrum requires us to have knowledge of abstract cognitive concepts and related impairments.

In the high school, as I pulled a program together that addressed problem solving and communication effectiveness, I realized that these abstract cognitive concepts had to be broken down into more manageable elements not only for the students but for the educators as well. Social-cognition is an area few of us study but most of us know how to utilize intuitively. Working with students whose weakness is primarily in their social-cognition requires us to become aware of *how we* succeed with that working knowledge.

Comfort came in being able to break down these loftier components into smaller pieces that both the students and I could relate to. My premise is that there are six components that are fundamental to our ability to gain skills in these two larger areas. My husband gave these six components (listed on the next page) the acronym "I LAUGH" so that we overburdened educators could have some hook on which to hang our budding knowledge. These concepts are not presented in any particular sequential order.

The I Laugh approach

An acronym for the pieces of communicative effectiveness *and* personal problem solving…

I=Initiating novel activities

L=Listening actively

A=Abstracting & inferencing

U=Understanding perspective

G=Gestalt: the big picture

H=Humor & Human Relatedness

The I LAUGH components were originally geared specifically towards helping create better problem solvers. However, as I explored further, I found that these same I LAUGH components contribute towards communicative success. What a relief to realize that the same set of concepts had direct application to the two most powerful elements for developing competence as we age: problem solving and effective communication.

Throughout the following chapters we will explore the I LAUGH components and show how to teach aspects of social knowledge in a more manageable way. At the same time it is important to recognize that these components, while unique, require synchronicity in order to achieve the higher knowledge and functional base that we are shooting for. ***It is essential that our teachings work not only to break down tasks for our students but to put them back together again!***

The I LAUGH approach is enlarged on the previous page for posting in classrooms and for reviewing with students. A worksheet beginning on page 18 is for older students (late middle school and above) to review to see if they can relate some of their strengths and weaknesses to the I LAUGH components.

Name _____ Date_____

SOLVING PROBLEMS BEFORE THEY BECOME PROBLEMS

1. What is the problem?

_____

2. What choices do you have to solve the problem?

1.A bad choice:	**2.** A good choice:	**3.** A good choice:

3. Write in possible consequences of each choice:

1.	**2.**	**3.**

1. What choice or choices are best to pick?_____

2. When are you going to start to solve your problem? (List time and/or date)_____

3. Where are you going to do this? (Location)

_____

4. Who do you need to talk to, to help? (Person)

_____

5. What are you going to say or ask?

_____
_____

Name _____ Date_____

THE ONE BIG RULE!

There is one big rule for problem solving:

The way you choose to solve your problem should result in either eliminating the problem or in minimizing problems.

If you have created a bigger or different problem, then...you did not solve your problem!

What is a problem you have had this past month???

What is the way you chose to solve it????

What are two other ways you could think of to solve it???? Be flexible!!!

1._____

2._____

Name _____ Date_____

Learning about Social Thinking and how it Relates to You!

We are working on:
1. Communicative effectiveness
2. Personal problem solving

To be successful at these requires you to understand each of the components listed below. After reading about each component, write some comments about how you see yourself performing with regard to these concepts.

a. <u>Taking Perspective</u>
This is the ability to think about your own and others' ideas and thoughts.

_____

_____

_____

_____

_____

page 2 Learning About Social Thinking and How it Relates to You!

b. Taking Initiative

This is the ability to start something new, whether it is a specific task or a conversation.

_____

_____

_____

_____

_____

c. Being a Good Listener: This is the ability to concentrate on what other people are talking about, even when it is not of great interest to you.

_____

_____

_____

_____

d. <u>Being able to Abstract and Infer:</u>
This is the ability to figure out what people are talking about when it is not clearly stated.

_____

_____

_____

_____

_____

e. <u>Gestalt</u>: Seeing the "big picture"-This is the ability to make a bigger sense out of the little things you have to deal with. For example, how do all the smaller pieces of information you read in a story connect to one big theme? What is the theme?

_____

_____

_____

_____

_____

Chapter 1: The I LAUGH APPROACH

Page 4 Learning About Social Thinking and How it Relates to You!

List 5 things that you do really well:

_____

_____

_____

_____

_____

Given the above review of the information, which of the above components give you the most trouble?

_____

_____

_____

Which would you like to work on first?

_____

_____

Which, do you think, are the easiest for you?

_____

_____

Summary of the I LAUGH APPROACH:

Persons with social-cognitive deficits have significant difficulties in their ability to effectively communicate and problem solve. These concepts are large and complicated. To work towards developing skills in both of these areas, the concepts need to be broken down into smaller, more tangible parts. The I LAUGH approach takes six aspects of higher order thinking and explores how each aspect contributes communicative effectiveness and personal-problem-solving. The chart on the following page summarizes what will be reviewed in the following chapters.

SUMMARY OF "I LAUGH" MODEL AND CORRESPONDING TREATMENT IDEAS

I LAUGH Components	I LAUGH Explanation	I LAUGH Treatment ideas
Communicative effectiveness & personal-problem solving = The I LAUGH model.	To help facilitate development with both **communication** and **problem solving,** we need to explore the pieces of these processes that can be explored more concretely. The "I LAUGH" acronym represents these pieces.	While communicative effectiveness and problem solving are our ultimate treatment goals, these are huge chunks. The total goal of treatment is to address the treatment ideas below, and then help the student see how each piece plays into the bigger whole of communication and problem solving. • Use the Problem Solving Framework to explore how the process is broken down. • Use Comic Strip Conversations (Carol Gray, 1994) to explore total communication.

I = INITIATING	**INITIATION** of any non-routine action including both communicative and physical activities.	• Build initiation into routines. • Establish time lines to get started with activities. • Build initiation into social stories and scripts. • Specifically teach how a student can "ask for help."
L = LISTENING WITH YOUR EYES AND BRAIN	**LISTENING**: In addition to hearing the words, listening involves actively participating through observation of the context and making logical connections in our heads to what it all means.	• Use visual strategies. • Check comprehension by asking the student to repeat the message. • Have student write out what he is to do. • Teach the idea of "listening with your eyes." Seeing what is going on around you connects to what is being said.
A = ABSTRACT AND INFERENTIAL LANGUAGE	**ABSTRACT AND INFERENTIAL LANGUAGE**: refers to both the figurative language used as well as the fact the communication itself is an abstract process requiring us to interpret multiple levels of information simultaneously and immediately.	• Teach the difference between figurative and literal language. • Teach prediction and inference (start by encouraging guess-making). • Teach vocabulary that is more abstract (e.g. emotions) from an experiential place. • Use Carol Gray's Colored Conversational Words to help explore the different levels of emotional meaning. • Teach about the different aspects of language that need to be interpreted (body language, facial expression, tone of voice, etc.)

Components	Explanation	Treatment Ideas
U = UNDERSTANDING PERSPECTIVE	**UNDERSTANDING PERSPECTIVE** is very complicated since most of us do it intuitively. We begin by understanding that we think about each other based on a variety of expectations and other factors, some of which change rapidly (e.g. facial expressions, tone of voice, words used, etc.) Most persons with Asperger Syndrome don't recognize the many layers of perspective taking. They then learn to do this more cognitively rather than intuitively, which is hard work!	• Teach what it means to "make impressions." • Teach recognition of their own emotions. • Teach recognition of others' emotional states and what others expect from you in those states. • Explore how rule based social skills help to maintain sense of perspective (e.g. turn-taking, asking questions, etc.). • Explore what expectations come to the context based on past memories, gender, age, present contextual cues, etc. • Explore reading comprehension through the changing perspectives of characters in books. • Pen pal to get an opportunity to explore relationships that can be "frozen" for exploration in the letters written.

Components	Explanation	Treatment Ideas
G = **GETTING THE BIG PICTURE (GESTALT)**	**GETTING THE BIG PICTURE (GESTALT)** refers to the fact that most folks with AS have a difficult time seeing how smaller pieces form into the larger whole, or how the larger concept breaks down into smaller pieces. This is the child who is given a set of directions and then told to get to work on the project…but it was never explained to them how the project and the instructions are linked. Confusion results. Difficulty seeing the big picture also relates to problems with organization and prioritizing.	• Buy and USE an academic planner to see how projects unfold over time. • Use visual imagery to demonstrate how the "whole" and the "pieces" work as one. • Have the student inference to break down tasks into smaller parts with some facilitating questions (use of written frameworks). • Work on organization and prioritizing using the brain rather than just making things look neat. • Prioritize home and school activities in the same planner. • Keep working on making guesses!
H = **HUMOR**	**HUMOR** – This is all too serious to be taken too seriously… We need to establish a relationship with these folks that we both enjoy. Use humor and warm relationships to actually teach the techniques and not as something that is offered after the lesson is complete.	• Teach when humor is appropriate and when it is not. • Laugh at your mistakes! • Use your own version of the rubber chicken!

Chapter 2

WHY CARE??

An attempt to answer a common question

For many students, the push to teach them skills related to social interaction leaves them scratching their heads and saying, "I don't care!" Parents frequently ask me what to do to help their children "see the light."

Perhaps part of the student's resistance is related to the external pressure to develop better "social skills" without the student understanding how each skill is part of the bigger picture of communicative success. Perhaps it is because the student is being told that the skills will help him make friends while he feels satisfied with his current social situation. And... perhaps it is because the student does not understand how social-cognition and related skills are critical for success across most of our daily settings, no matter how mundane.

On the pages at the end of this chapter are worksheets I use with students to help them develop an understanding of how social-cognition plays out across their day beyond just the outwardly social elements such as conversations.

These worksheets help me set a tone of understanding in our therapy sessions. The concepts we explore will help students access information they want and need (e.g. requesting help from teachers, interviewing for jobs, minimizing family friction) and will not be limited to those that enable happy social adventures.

Contrary to what socially savvy caregivers think, social groups do not necessarily initially imply social fun! For many of our students, coming together to relate at a more personal level in a "social group" is a cause for great anxiety. For younger students who have significant attentional, sensory and interpretive issues, this can be the most challenging part of their day! Appreciate the stress students in the groups can be experiencing. Help them explore every part of learning, including why they should care….and most do!

Summary of Chapter 2, Why Care:

Many students with social-cognitive deficits have difficulty understanding the true nature of their disability. In an attempt to help, caregivers often explain that participating in therapy will help students "make friends" or be "more like others." However, students often exclaim, "I don't care!" when encouraged to take a more active role in developing their "social skills." The first step in working with these students is to help them realize that their social thinking and related skills deficit impacts more than their world of friendships (which is significant in itself!). Namely, a solid understanding of social thinking allows them to develop independence.

Name_____ Date_____

Why Care????

(For 5th graders and up)

Why care what someone thinks of you...?

_____

_____

What is important for you to do at school and at home? Only list 4.

1._____

_____

2._____

_____

3._____

_____

4._____

_____

Which of the above have to do with:

 -Talking to another person?

 -Thinking about another person?

 -Understanding another person?

Page 2 Why Care?

Go back to what you wrote on the first page and circle the number of the ones that involve talking, thinking about or understanding other people.

Which of these have to do with:
-Thinking about yourself?
-Completing something that someone else will look at?

Circle the numbers that involve thinking about yourself or completing something for someone else.

How many of the above numbers have you circled? _____

The circled numbers have to do with anything where you have to think about yourself and other people. Thinking about people has to do with social thinking. Social thinking is a lot more than making and keeping friends....it also has to do with understanding history, social studies, English, playing on teams in PE, and developing responsibilities so you can grow up and move out of the house one day!

Page 3 Why Care?

Let's explore when else you have to think about another person...

What type of social thinking is needed for:

Reading a book about people?

Playing sports?

Doing responsibilities around the house?

Social thinking is what we are working on in the therapy groups...the more you practice it, the easier it will be for you to do!

Circle the ones that involve social thinking:

a. Ride a bike
b. Say things to keep people cool, calm and collected
c. Turn in your homework
d. Write a paragraph about something you just read
e. Make yourself lunch
f. Make someone else lunch
g. Take a shower
h. Comb your hair
i. Carry your backpack
j. Do a chore around the house

Page 4 Why Care?

k. Argue
l. Play a video game by yourself
m. Solving a problem where you have to talk to someone
n. Hanging with your friends at lunch
o. Being by yourself
p. Talking to your teacher
q. Talking to your parents

Review the letters you circled. How many DON'T have to do with social thinking???

What do you think about that???

Name _____

Date _____

<u>Why should you care about others????</u>
(For use with elementary school children)

Name 3 things you can do for other people...

1. _____

_____

2. _____

_____

3. _____

_____

Name 3 things others people can do for you (that do not have to do with buying you things!)

1. _____

_____

2. _____

_____

3. _____

Page 2 Why Care About Others?

Why do you think we even bother to be with or think about other people?

Thinking about people has to do with social thinking. Social thinking is a lot more than making and keeping friends….it also has to do with understanding history, social studies, English, playing on teams in PE, and developing responsibilities so you can grow up and take care of yourself!

Below is a list of things that we do a lot. Circle the ones that make you think about other people or yourself while you are doing them.

   a. Riding a bike
   b. Saying things to keep people happy
   c. Turning in your homework
   d. Writing a paragraph about something you just read
   e. Making yourself a snack
   f. Making someone else a snack
   g. Taking a shower
   h. Combing your hair
   i. Carrying your backpack
   j. Doing a chore around the house
   k. Arguing
   l. Playing a video game by yourself

Page 3 Why Care About Others?

m. Solving a problem where you have to talk to someone
n. Hanging with your friends at lunch
o. Being by yourself
p. Talking to your teacher

HOW MANY DON'T HAVE TO DO WITH SOCIAL THINKING???

Just about everything we do involves thinking about people in one way or another. Learning about how to think about people is a good way to help people to like you and want to be with you!

"I LAUGH"

Chapter 3

INITIATION....

LET'S GET STARTED!

"Initiation" is a concept that means starting a behavior that is not
routine. This difficulty can occur with novel verbal and/or
physical tasks. It is confusing how high-level students who are
generally quite verbal can have difficulty initiating a verbal task.
Once they are comfortable talking, these students can talk
endlessly! The key here is in the fact that the task to be initiated is
not routine. Social greetings, while very routine to neuro-typical
people, can be quite anxiety provoking for our students. The
words may stay the same, yet the context and person receiving
them constantly change. The same goes for homework. The
routine assignment (spelling words or math facts) can usually be fit
into the schedule and completed far more reliably than the month
long projects. Our students have great difficulty getting started
with projects that are to be worked on across time!

Language tasks related to initiation include some of the following:

1. Asking for help, especially from a teacher!

2. Determining what words to say to formulate the message.

3. Determining when is the appropriate time to say the words.

About Asking For Help:

A bright young man was having difficulty getting through his college courses. I met him shortly after he had dropped out of college. I asked him how he would ask for help at school and he informed me that he "never, ever asked for help" throughout his entire academic career. When I asked him why (after giving him many different options to chose from) he responded that he did not want to "look stupid." I was meeting with him to help him prepare for his first week at work at a job in a local chain store. I discussed with him the expectations that go with starting a new job, namely that you must ask at least five questions a day for the first few days that you are on the job. I explained how this is a situation where they expect that you don't know the information, and they allow you a window of time in which to learn it. Asking for help during that time is essential for keeping the job! Given that information, the young man was successful in asking specific questions to gain access to information. He recently received a promotion!

Teaching children strategies to request help is one of the first tasks when working with students with social-cognitive deficits. Some students are comfortable doing this on their own in the classroom, but most are not. There is a big difference between talking in class about the information in your head and actually asking for help. As we observe these students in their classrooms we need to sort out these different types of verbalizations.

Some students do not like the attention called to them when they raise their hands; they need to begin by establishing proximity with the teacher by standing next to her desk.

Evaluate the current status of the student's ability to initiate by:

1. Observing their present methods in the classroom; some have no strategy other than to squirm in their chairs, make noises or shut down.

2. Questioning the child as to his preferences on how to seek help.

3. Writing a goal and related objective in the IEP to address the situation.

4. Developing a sequenced strategy for helping the child develop a more successful technique.

An example of a sequenced outline for
"ASKING FOR HELP"

For students who do not realize what to do,
or are unsure:

1. Look around at what other students are doing and see if you can figure out what is supposed to happen next.

2. If that didn't help, raise your hand and look towards the teacher.

3. Think of the question you need to ask in your head. Rehearse it.

4. When the teacher comes over, show her the place on the paper you are stuck and then ask her the question you have in your head.

5. Watch the teacher's face as she talks or watch what she writes on your paper to show you the answer.

6. If the answer still doesn't make sense to you, tell the teacher you are still confused.

7. When she is done, look at her and say "Thank you."

8. Get back to work!

In addition to breaking information down into sequences, allowing students to use *visual cuing cards is also a good idea.* If the child is not fidgety, an index card can be affixed to his desk that cues him to ask for help when confused.

Not knowing what words to say:

Another concept that is difficult to fathom is that these verbal students do not know what words to say (difficulty with language formulation) when they are in a "forced communication" type situation. This is very different from just being able to "download" information from your brain for the amusement of others.

When I work with older students/young adults I will often find that they can describe to me who they need to speak to and what the content of that discussion should be about. However, when I ask them how they are going to approach the person and what they are going to say, they often respond that they don't know.

A simple, useful strategy is for them to write on a sheet of paper the answers to the following questions:

1. Who are you going to speak to?
2. When are you going to speak to them?
3. Where are you going to speak to them?
4. What are you going to say?

Breaking down the task and writing it out in this way provides a concrete structure that is missing in their otherwise knowledgeable minds. A worksheet is provided on page 49 to use with students for this reason. In Chapter 1 on page 16 the "Solving Problems Before They Become Problems" worksheet has these four questions as the final task in problem solving personal problems. It is one thing to conceptually solve problems in our heads, but a whole different task to actually follow it through in real life. These questions help guide through that process.

Language that is used to establish a relationship with another person requires social knowledge as well as organization of thought. This blends over to aspects that will be covered later under the topics of "abstract and inferential language" as well as "getting the big picture." It is important to note that not having the words to say, at the moment you need to say them, may stem from a number of causes, including difficulty with initiation.

Not knowing when to say the words!

Blurting out information at the wrong time is a common problem. This would certainly not be referred to as a "lack of initiation," but more "lack of appropriate initiation."

There are 3 types of blurting:

1. Students who fail to monitor the social structure of the classroom or other setting; they tend to talk when the mood strikes regardless without full consideration as to whether the teacher is providing a classroom lecture versus encouraging a classroom discussion.

2. Students who have difficulty realizing that the teacher is not speaking to them alone. Some of my older clients will tell me they did not realize that they were part of the class group until they were in their teens. For this type of student the teacher exists solely to teach *him*, regardless of the fact 25 other kids may share the room. While all people tend to be somewhat egocentric, our students with social cognitive deficits have difficulty determining the intentions of others around them.

3.   Students whose minds wander among concepts discussed resulting in tangential thinking. Saying a comment that is loosely related to the topic at hand, even when it is said at a fairly appropriate time may throw the class off track.

There are also times when a student does not blurt out; he simply does not speak.

Some students will tell you they know they need to speak in the class group or to a teacher but they just can't figure out when that time should be (everyone always looks busy!). These students do well with an approach called scripting that is described below.

INITIATION is more than just getting the word or project moving forward. It also has a planning/logistics element to it. The reader may want to refer to chapter 7 "Getting the Big Picture" for more information on these types of problems.

What can we do to help????

Create an expectation of initiation.
- ❑ Establish an environment that encourages and rewards initiation. Educators need to understand how truly challenging this can be for some students.

Build initiation into routines!
- ❑ Discuss with the child why the initiation of language is important in such a routine.
- ❑ Consistently follow up on initiation routines that have been established, whether this includes initial

social greetings or encouraging the student to ask for help.

If the person is a very delayed responder….

- ❑ Set a specific time limit that is a reasonable response time.
- ❑ Write a social story to review expectations for time allowances in verbal replies. Carol Gray developed the notion of Social Stories to help the child process interactions and expectations more thoroughly. She describes Social Stories as having 3 elements to foster students' understanding of contexts:

  a. Descriptive sentences: sentences that describe the concrete environment.
  b. Perspective sentences: sentences that describe the perspective of persons involved in the social story context.
  c. Directive sentences: sentences that more clearly define the student's expected role in the social story context.

  For the reader to become more familiar with Carol Gray's work I refer you to the bibliography in the back of this book and the chapter she wrote in the book "Higher Functioning Adolescents and Young Adults with Autism" (Fullerton, Stratton, Coyne and Gray; 1996).
- ❑ Work with the child on language formulation and organization tasks to help him more easily establish initiation.

Not knowing When To Speak Out In Class:

For the blurter:

❑ Enlighten the student about the hidden "social structures" that exist in group settings. Teach him to be able to tell the difference between times that all kids can talk, versus small group discussions, versus teacher led discussions. Familiarize him with the concept of the rhetorical question. This becomes particularly important during school assemblies.

For the quiet student:

❑ **Script out speaking opportunities.**
Scripting is a procedure that we use to approximate what an interaction might look like, much as we do when writing a script for a play. However, it is really important to recognize that there is more to a script than the words. We also need to script out the body language and facial expression we want the student to observe. Scripting can be done either by parents or professionals. The script below might be one a parent would write before sending her child off to school.

(Script example:)
Joe needs to talk to the school secretary:
Joe: *Approaches the secretary and stands in front of her desk.*
Secretary: *Looks up at Joe.*

> *Joe*: (*cued to speak by her eye contact, pulls out a note from his mother and says*)
> "*I need a pass to leave early today.*"
> *Secretary:* *Directs him to fill his name in a book and writes him a pass.*
> *Joe*: *Looks at the secretary's face and says Thank you.*"

When it comes to initiation, the student cannot do it all!

While students are working on increasing their understanding and comfort levels for dealing with initiation, they will need assistance seeking help, relaying information etc. Very often when I work with school personnel they will point out that a particular teacher or aide is available to assist the child, but that the child never asks for assistance. ***Teaching those who work with students about the difficulties surrounding initiating is really important. However, at first we can't expect the student to seek out the teacher! We need the teacher to seek out the student.***

George, a high school student I had just started working with had such poor initiation that he was virtually selectively mute when on the school campus. When the student failed a class, I asked if he ever went to tutorial. He responded that he went every day. When I asked the teacher why George failed since he regularly attended the tutorial session, the teacher replied that he came but he always read the newspaper! The student did not have the strategy to ask for help and hoped that proximity to the teacher would gain him access to getting help. In this case it did not work. After that experience I wrote a note to each of the student's teachers explaining his difficulty initiating communication, especially when seeking guidance. Given that extra bit of knowledge, his educators became much more interactive, by offering him their guiding hand. The student eventually became proficient at standing near the teacher's desk when he needed help.

Another high school student named Mac had a resource period in Special Education. However, he continued to have great difficulty in his English class. The teacher and aide pointed out that they were there for him whenever he needed them. Mac responded during his IEP meeting that he was just "lazy." I worked with Mac and his family in my clinic and during the meeting I asked him if he ever sat around the house, was he a "couch potato"? Mac replied that he was always busy working on homework. I clarified that a person who works hard at home, but has trouble seeking information in school is not "lazy", but perhaps "overwhelmed" by the confusions in his day. The IEP team decided that each day, Mac came to the resource period, he should fill out a form called "I'm overwhelmed today by…" where he could write out specific classes and assignments that he did not understand. The teacher in the resource room could then understand his needs and come to him with assistance.

The above examples point out that difficulty with initiation continues into young adulthood for some people. This is clearly not a difficulty only associated with young children. The more anxiety a situation produces, the more difficult it will be to initiate communication in that context.

Modifications need to be made in the environment to help the student gain access to information. At the same time we can be working on strategies to help the student feel more comfortable in employing his communication skills.

Ideas for Goals and Objectives related to Initiation:

Goal: Student will initiate communication to request assistance or will participate in social interactions with initial cues.

Objective 1: The student will ask for help or for clarification, given a specific cueing system, 80% of the time.

Objective 2: The student will participate in reviewing social stories and scripting strategies sessions 90% of the time.

Objective 3: The student will use a scripted strategy to successfully interact with another person, 80% of the time.

Summary Chapter 3-Initiation

"Initiation" is a concept that means having to start a behavior that is not routine.

As with all skills, working towards increasing initiation has two components:

1. *What the student needs to learn:*
   To increase his skill and comfort in this area given the above strategies.

2. *What the parents and professionals have to do*:
   Facilitate helping the student communicate across environments. Primarily this means that merely being available to a student is often not enough. Helping to facilitate a student's appropriate communication with you is a great first step towards decreasing the student's anxiety and opening the door to the idea that you are "safe" to be approached in the future.

Name _____ Date _____

DOING THAT TALKING THANG!

1. Why are you going to talk to them?

_____

2. Who are you going to talk to?

_____

3. Where are you going to talk to them?

_____

4. When are you going to talk to them?

_____

5. What are you going to say??

_____

_____

_____

"I LAUGH"

Chapter 4

LISTENING AND ATTENTION

...Through our Eyes and Ears

Listening is more than hearing! Many persons with social-cognitive deficits, particularly those on the autism spectrum, were initially perceived to have a hearing loss when very young because of their frequent lack of attention to the sounds in their environment. Other students may have a heightened arousal to sound, startle easily and are uncomfortable in noisy environments. Usually the physical mechanism for hearing the sound is intact, although like with any population, there is a chance for hearing loss and deafness with this group as well.   However, the mechanism for processing the sounds in the brain is not nearly as efficient as it should be. Thus, professionals talking about this aspect of the disability may refer to an "auditory processing problem" or a "central auditory processing disorder," commonly labeled as CAPD. Audiologists have the most specific tests to give related to this disability. There are tests for auditory processing that can be given by psychologists and speech language pathologists, with a mixed degree of accuracy. I worked with a freshman in high school that had a tremendous delay in processing language, which I observed just by speaking with him. Although he scored "in the low average" on the auditory processing tests provided by the psychologist, this score was not low enough to qualify him for related services. Unfortunately, I found that he was not given timed tests of processing. He would eventually give the appropriate answer, sometimes taking up to 5 minutes to respond. Unfortunately the pace of our world leaves this type of auditory processor in the dust.

The research demonstrates that students on the autism spectrum also have a poor response to activities that require rapid attentional shifts (Wainwright-Sharp & Bryson, 1993) and diminished ability to comprehend spoken instructions (Boucher & Lewis, 1989). Many parents question why their children appear to have such a poor auditory memory in one setting, then show a terrific ability to repeat verbatim what was said on a TV show via delayed echolalia. My best guess on this is that there appears to be a difference between recall of a superficially processed message, and storage and recall of a deeply processed message.

Folks with quirky attention spans:

In addition to generally having true deficits in processing the language, this population is also frequently diagnosed with some aspect of attention deficit. Are they related? You bet! It is difficult to attend to what you do not understand or to auditorily process ideas that you don't relate to (like gestalt oriented or abstract oriented concepts). At the same time, our students have great internal creativity. Their minds take them to places they find interesting, often in spite of the activities that are going on in front of them.

I worked with two high school boys with high-functioning autism; the lesson of the day was about teaching directed eye-contact. I was attempting to get the boys involved in shared eye-contact. Despite my best attempts, whomever I was speaking directly to looked at ME while the other student looked away. My appeals to have both boys participate in the lesson simultaneously went unheeded. As I continued, I noticed that one of them looked away and laughed. I said, "Frank, where are you right now?" and he looked at me and replied, "In Las Vegas playing the slot machines!"

No matter how experienced the clinician or sophisticated the therapy equipment, at times it is difficult to compete with the inner, exciting world of the person who lives on the autism spectrum! (I admit to occasional jealousy of their ability to be self-entertained!) So once again there are no clear boundaries to auditory processing vs. attention deficit vs. life. As we frequently find ourselves professionally, we are in a bit of a muddle.

Finally, we also have to deal with the sophistication of the persons we are working with. Virtually all of our students are clever individuals. They don't always appreciate our "nagging" which we try to disguise as "therapeutic interventions." As they get older (high-school age), they can act as if they are listening by nodding their heads and establishing eye-contact with the teacher. If we try to cover our bases by asking a student, "did you understand what I was talking about?" He inevitably will answer, "yes." **Don't trust 'em!!** Effective listening by a student when part of a larger group is even worse!

Example 1:

A freshman high-school boy was flunking science. I stayed after school to assist him with seeking help from his science teacher. She asked him if he had gotten the information about a specific mountain range; he indicated he had not by looking confused. The teacher then launched into a fairly lengthy explanation of the mountain range as my student stood there looking blankly at his teacher. I interrupted towards the beginning of her explanation to ask my student if he wanted to take notes since this required a lot of listening. He replied he did not need to. At the conclusion of the teacher's lecture, I asked him if he understood what she said (I didn't!). He replied that he had. **When I asked him to repeat the basic ideas he could not recall one!** *At that point I informed the student and the teacher that unless he was writing down what she said, or she was writing notes for him, there was little point in saying it!*

Example 2:
A 7-year-old, very high-level boy with Asperger syndrome participated in his classroom circle time. The boy loved reading and sat attentively as his teacher read. As soon as she began to talk to the group of children after concluding the book, the boy's eyes wandered around the room and he began to talk to himself, using animated gestures that in no way related to any activity the teacher was discussing. This same boy could have very clear and coherent discussions with one other person, but he had almost no skills for listening as part of a group!

What can we do to help?

Most of the strategies we can employ both at home and at school come from modifications we can provide in the environment.

1. Provide visual information to compliment spoken information. Boucher and Lewis (1989) demonstrated that written instructions provided for persons with autism helped to overcome difficulties processing spoken and visually demonstrated instructions. Use overheads in the classroom for this purpose because they present the information at the time it is said. They can also be placed at a child's desk once the lecture is finished. Visual cues should be used regardless of a student's measured intelligence or language/reading skills.

A teacher of a 6-year-old boy with Asperger Syndrome and behavior problems informed the mother that she would not use a pictured or written schedule with the student because he "was too smart" and it would make him feel bad!

2. Asking the student to repeat what you want him to do, rather than simply asking him if he understands.

3. "Write out instructions and make them available at the child's work-desk. If this is for an older student and a previous discussion has reviewed the instructions, it is preferable at times to try and have the student write out the steps. This encourages the student to continue to work at auditory processing as well as to use skills related to understanding the gestalt.

There are also emerging techniques to work on auditory processing skills that the team working with the student should be aware of:

4. Traditional Speech and Language services provide therapy focused on increasing auditory comprehension. The use of Lindamood-Bell auditory comprehension programs such as "Visualize-Verbalize" (www.lindamoodbell.com) has been successful with this population.

5. Computer programs are now being professionally developed to assist with processing the auditory signal. *FastForword* is an intensive computer program designed to slow down the auditory signal to help the student to learn to process it at a slower speed, and then gradually the auditory signal is sped back up through a series of games and maneuvers the student plays over time. (FastForword, www.scientificlearning.com)

6. Auditory Integration Training programs have been demonstrated to aid in the ability to attend to sound signals

thereby assisting the student's ability to process sounds. This program is non-intrusive and does not require great attentional intensity from the participant. Many of my families (not all) have noted benefits from having their students participate in auditory integration training. However, some families report that the benefits do not last over a lengthy period of time (many years), in which case they find it necessary to repeat the procedure. More information can be found on the internet using a search for "Auditory Integration Training."

7. Become familiar with Dr. Mel Levine's work on Attention Controls. He has a very logical approach towards helping students develop their own understanding of their deficits related to attending and controlling their attention. (EPS, 1999).

8. I have also found it helpful to work with students to define what it means to "listen." This chapter is named "listening and attention through our eyes and ears" because the deficits with auditory processing can be diminished if the student knows how to "listen with his eyes." This requires him to learn to attend to subtle cues in the environment as well as to use his eyes to "lip read," a skill that most of us do naturally to some degree.

Summary for Listening and Attention:

Most, if not all, students with deficits in social-cognition demonstrate some form of auditory processing deficit. Techniques to help the student better attend to his present environment include modifications to the environment as well as direct services that can be delivered to the student to help sharpen his listening/attending skills.

Modifications to the environment may include:

1. Present visually written or icon based instructions.

2. Ask the student to repeat instructions in his own words rather than accept his assurance that he understands.

Procedures to help the student increase his ability to attend/listen to spoken information may include:

1. Traditional speech and language therapy programs.

2. Computer driven intensive participation programs such as *FastForward*.

3. Have the student participate in an Auditory Integration program.

4. Teach the student about his attentional deficits, so he can be more familiar with his needs and have strategies to compensate.

"I LAUGH"

Chapter 5

Abstract and inferential thinking…

I mean what I say,

but I don't say what I mean!!!

Abstract and inferential language requires us to consider what is not clearly stated. It often demands us to link together knowledge that was previously isolated. Language that is stated implicitly, that requires little interpretation, is referred to as "literal." Persons with social-cognitive deficits tend to be more literal in their understanding and use of language; they are often described as "concrete thinkers" having difficulty inferring meaning from contextual as well as verbal messages.

Abstract and inferential thinking can be broken into at least 4 basic components:

1. Inferring information
2. Dealing with abstract language
3. Formulating language and ideas
4. Fully understanding the meaning of non-verbal communication

1. Inferring information:

Inferencing has to do with making guesses, both verbal and non-verbal. Interpreting messages is a chancy prospect, requiring us to "take what we know about a situation and make a guess." Many of our students have told me that they "hate guessing," preferring to deal with information that is "rock solid."

Brian was an adolescent with High-Functioning Autism. He was answering questions as part of being given the Test Of Problem Solving (LinguiSystems, Inc., 1991). One question had to do with a paragraph that explores how a child feels after his pet has died. Brian was asked, "Why do you think burying a pet is important to some young children?" Brian's answer: **"So that you don't trip over him in your house."**

As we advance through childhood it is expected that our inferential reasoning skills blossom rapidly. Activities in the classroom that foster inferencing are referred to as "critical thinking" tasks. These are considered to be tasks that, once completed, demonstrate a thorough grasp of the concepts being taught. The educational curriculum in the United States, beginning around 3rd and 4th grades focuses a lot of attention on critical thinking activities since they demonstrate a student's ability to process and integrate information. Even for our high-level students with social-cognitive deficits, assignments related to critical thinking activities can be overwhelming. Given that many of our students perform very well on both standardized achievement and intelligence testing, it is confusing to teachers and psychologists that such a gap exists between the high achievement the test scores represent and the low performance the student demonstrates in class. To add to the confusion, students in elementary school who are frustrated by assignments requiring critical thinking or language formulation are prone to "act out" in class, making them appear "behaviorally disturbed."

The task of inferencing is complicated because it is the result of at least three high-level processes:

1. <u>Gestalt thinking</u>: which requires one to grasp the entirety of a concept and be able to organize or segment what we observe (described in chapter 7).
2. <u>Prediction</u>: the ability to make a guess after considering and organizing the gestalt based information.
3. <u>Sequencing</u>: being able to determine the natural order of events.

Inferencing is a task of varying complexity. The most basic level is "concrete inferences." These are guesses that are based on relatively stable information (information that is grounded in facts). For example, if I see gray clouds and wet pavement I will guess that I should wear my raincoat outside. The most advanced level is that of "emotional inferencing" whereby guesses and predictions are based on relatively unstable information, information about human emotion and reactions. For example, a student might think "Will the teacher act the same way today as he did yesterday when I asked him for help?"

Inferencing is required across many tasks in the classroom itself:

1. **Reading comprehension** of literature requires us to hook together multiple concepts while following characters' emotions and situational problems in much the same way that we need to track real-life relationships. Reading comprehension is chock full of inferencing!

2. **Social Studies and History** assignments that require a student to "compare and contrast"

3. **Science curriculum often requires prediction,** even if they are based on scientific factual knowledge. There are different types of predictions and it appears that predictions based on concrete scientific knowledge are less complex predictions than figuring out how people feel or think (social cognitive predictions).

4. **Creating schedules** to assist with time management. Many of our students are woefully unorganized, yet they function best in the concrete world of routine and structure. A highly structured world alleviates a lot of inferencing! However, creating an effective, structured schedule requires loads of gestalt thinking and predicting. Thus, these students are NOT usually good at managing their own time effectively. This is discussed further with the example of "Tina's schedule" in Chapter 7.

5. **Interacting with peers in the classroom,** particularly during the dreaded "group work" assignment can be a great challenge.

6. **Problem Solving** to avoid the further development of personal problems requires abstract thinking. The choices we evaluate to complete a problem-solving task require us to infer relationships both between the stated problem and the possible choices, as well as between the choices and potential consequences. See the problem-solving sheet on page 16.

While inferencing required in the academic context can be taxing to our students with social-cognitive deficits, it cannot be avoided. Our students must learn to have some mastery with this skill if they are to develop independence later in life. At the same time, we cannot merely assume that because these students are bright, they will get it if they "just work harder!" Helping the students by guiding their thinking through a set of facilitating questions is ideal. This strategy is reviewed in Chapter 7. Practicing this skill in more individualized or small group sessions is also useful.

2. Dealing with Abstract Language

Abstract language is the use of words in such a way their literal and actual meanings are generally two very different entities. For some very high-level language users with social-cognitive deficits, abstract language can pose no extra burden. But, for the majority of our students, who are always in search of the concrete meaning, abstract language can appear as huge hurdles in the path of deciphering the language code. Idioms, metaphors, similes, sarcasm and poetry are a few of the more notable aspects of abstract language which can send our students into pools of confusion. In schools, abstract language is often referred to as "figurative language." I teach students that figurative language means that they have to "figure-it-out!"

Tad, a 7-year-old science-oriented boy, was singing "This Land is Your Land" in class and made this comment to his mom about the phrase "a ribbon of highway": "The song is so dumb! I never heard of a highway that you couldn't drive a truck on!"

Word groups such as "idioms" can be highly repetitive and therefore more easily learned. Teaching "idiomatic" lessons on a weekly basis allows a student to explore the difference between literal and non-literal meanings. The lessons can be a lot of fun.

They provide an opportunity to use humor while allowing the student to understand why a group of words such as "has the cat got your tongue?" means "why aren't you talking?" Idiomatic dictionaries are available in bookstores and often give some history as to how the expressions gained their meaning.

With respect to word meanings, persons with social-cognitive deficits may focus on limited aspects of word meanings. Single words that have multiple meanings can really throw a student. Words that have been learned in a narrow emotional framework can also cause distress.

Jack was a 16–year-old who was learning about the process of problem solving. When I would ask Jack about a specific problem that needed to be analyzed, he would put his fingers in his ears and put his head under the desk. He carried on like this for a number of weeks. Finally, I realized that Jack was reacting to the specific use of the word "problem." For whatever historical reason, he had developed an extreme dislike for that specific word. I said to Jack, "You don't like it when I say the word 'problem.' Problems can be very serious but most of the situations we are talking about are very minor, such as returning an overdue book to the library. When we are talking about minor problems, let's call them 'glitches.'" Jack agreed to this change in terminology and was able to complete the lessons while staying upright in his chair!

The *CONTEXT* in which a message is being said is another variable that carries a lot of interpretive meaning. Persons with social-cognitive deficits often fail to fully consider how the context may affect the meaning of the message.

Individual or small group therapy with a speech language pathologist is a good resource for helping students learn more about abstract language comprehension and use. Resource teachers can also explore how this language impacts reading comprehension.

Helping to educate teachers or other caregivers about the complexities of interpreting abstract and inferential language in the classroom is also a must. While we encourage the students to gain a better grasp of these concepts through our direct teaching and by allowing them more time to analyze and interpret the material, we must not forget that they have a neurological deficit that will continue to impact their learning. In the environment in which they are to succeed, an attitude of understanding and encouragement is possible only when the caregivers have some understanding of this very *abstract* disability!

3. Formulating Language and Ideas:

The idea of pulling out something from nothing is the fun of language. Spoken language is a sophisticated process requiring us to organize our thoughts, determine appropriate word choice, apply words in grammatically correct units called sentences, and organize the sentences into a coherent set of verbal thoughts or paragraphs. The above steps require us to retrieve information in our brain and formulate it through our mouth with split-second precision. It is a neurological dance that is mind-boggling!

Certain aspects of this dance seem easier than others to persons with social-cognitive deficits. Highly verbal students are generally superior at word choice and grammar. Areas of deficits relate to organization (see Chapter 7 on Gestalt processing) and language formulation, which are both spoken and written. Many students on my caseload have difficulty starting a message. When they open their mouths to speak, they often falsely start and revise; the same holds true for written language. Between the fine motor demands of writing and the language formulation demands, the overall written language process can break down significantly for our students, even those who appear to be "verbally gifted."

For some students, language formulation difficulties are the result of word retrieval deficits. Language formulation is the process of thinking of a concept in your head and then quickly and efficiently retrieving and using words to produce language to express the concept. Poor language organizational skills can also hamper the formulation process. Useful tools for teaching students internal and external structures for organization are Venn diagrams, word webbing, and topic mapping.

Through my clinical experience, I have observed many students that have tremendous difficulty asking questions to people, while maintaining a conversation. It is not always that the student lacks information from which to ask questions; he may simply not know how to turn the information into a question from which he can move forward in the conversation.

Peter was an 18-year-old young man who had come to my office for an intake interview, in which I asked him about his development. After some time passed, I stopped my interview and asked him to take on the role of interviewing me. I cued him that as he was in my office, he could look around and learn a lot about me from which he could ask me questions. He looked at pictures of my family and my husband, who was playing trombone. Peter said, "I know you have a family" and "I know your husband plays trombone." I asked him how he could take that information and generate questions from which he could conduct the interview. He replied, "I don't know!"

Writing out our old familiar "Wh-" questions (e.g., Who, What, When, Where, Why and How) helps our students create a structure for their information. I often write the "Wh-" questions on index cards and we lay them out on the table in front of the student. One young man told me how helpful the cards were for him. He explained that he carried a picture of them in his head and mentally looked at them while in conversation. He also expressed the hope that with practice he could generate the questions automatically because this process took time!

Before entering into a social conversation, discuss the hidden meanings of why we participate in them:

When asked why we participate in conversations, our students respond that it's "to gain information." While this is partly true, it ignores the personal connection established in a communicative relationship. Teach students about the "underlying meaning" of social communication. S*how your communicative partner you are interested in HIM.*

Help your students realize that conversations have a hidden expectation, that they allow people to show their communicative partners that they "care about each other." Three ways in which a person can show that they care:

1. Ask questions about their partner's area of interest.
2. Establish and maintain appropriate non-verbal communication (e.g., not yawning when they are talking).
3. Make comments about their partner's interests.

The entire entry into the social communicative process is abstract!!! I teach students to begin a conversation by observing not by speaking. We observe a person to recall what we may remember about him as well as to consider his current personal state. Advancing into a conversation requires us to:

1. Observe the Person.
   How old is the person? Is the person wearing anything that would indicate his areas of interest (a shirt with a sports team logo, etc.)?

2. Determine what that person may want to talk about.
   We have different communicative expectations depending on the age or gender of a specific person. The students

need to explore that end. Why wouldn't a 30-year-old woman not want to talk about a child's TV show at length? What would a preschooler want to talk about?

3. <u>Formulate a question about the person's area of interest.</u>
Once zoned in on a particular topic of exploration, what question can you ask the other person to show your interest?

Worksheets on upcoming pages help students explore the utility of "small talk" as a tool for learning more about a person to help them zero in on conversational topics. The worksheets guide a person's thinking through the process of initially engaging with another person.

This does not mean that they should not have an opportunity to discuss their own area of interests as well, as their partner should share a similar interest in them. However, conversations require a careful weaving of information exchanged, keeping it balanced between both who's speaking and what topics they are speaking about. This is an important but difficult lesson for some of our students who can talk endlessly about their one topic of interest, but are saddened that they have no one left in their circle of friends who is willing to listen to them. More on how to think about other people is covered in Chapter 6, on Understanding Perspective.

Not all conversations share the same purpose: social versus formal conversations

Endlessly breaking down what we take for granted is the task of the caregiver working with persons with social-cognitive deficits. While it is always important to consider the interests and emotional state of the communicative partner, the type of conversation one engages in is different based on the purpose of the conversation. I review with students the following:

1. <u>Social conversations:</u>

Social conversations are for the purpose of establishing and/or maintaining a social relationship. We do this to enjoy the company of other people, to develop a deeper friendship or to simply be polite when you are caught in a situation that requires a social exchange regardless of whether you are really interested in talking (e.g. a graduation ceremony, a religious gathering, etc.). In social conversations we often begin with *small talk* which is a rapid-fire exchange of questions and answers about a number of different topics. The purpose of this is to gather information about the other person relatively quickly. This guides us towards a common interest on which we can begin a discussion around which we exchange questions and comments about one topic.

2. <u>*Formal conversations:*</u>

Formal conversations are for the purpose of exchanging information about a pre-set topic. For example: a business meeting, the need to clarify information with a teacher, or to request a specific action from a parent. In this type of conversation it is still appropriate to begin with social greetings, but generally one of the participants will make a direct statement about the topic that needs to be discussed. For example: "Would you please tell me how to write a bibliography for the report you assigned?" In this case, there is little need for small talk and a great need to maintain the specific topic under discussion by asking questions, answering questions and making relevant comments.

NAME_____ DATE_____Page 1

TO START TO GET TO KNOW SOMEONE:

Start with small talk

Small talk consists of those little questions you ask to find out general information about a person. Often the topic changes pretty rapidly. Why do you think we engage in small talk?

Step 1: Before you start talking, look at the person.

Are they wearing anything that indicates a hobby or interest (a t-shirt with a topic on it, a pin, or special jewelry)?

What is their age/sex?

Step 2: Given what you see or remember, about what might they be interested in talking?

1. _____

2. _____

3. _____

Page 2   To start to get to know someone

Step 3: What questions would you ask to start to engage in small talk?

1. _____
2. _____
3. _____

MOVING ON TO A CONVERSATION:

A conversation is a deeper discussion where you stay with one topic for a while, with each person taking turns to talk about the same topic. This is called "turn-taking."

- The conversation usually starts by one person making a comment or asking a question of the other.
- Each person can then add a comment or ask a question of the other to keep the conversation going.
- If the topic discussed is of interest to Person A, then Person A should ask a question of Person B about one of their areas of interest when the original topic "wears out." You have learned a bit about that person by engaging in the small talk above, so you can think of a question that is geared towards them.
- Passing the conversational topic back and forth is different from just turn-taking.

Why are conversations important to friendships?

_____
_____

Page 3   To start to get to know someone

What is Turn-taking?

_____

_____

_____

Why is it important?

_____

_____

_____

What is "passing a conversational topic"?

_____

_____

_____

Why is it important?

_____

_____

_____

Name_____ Date_____

COOL COMMENTS FOR COOL FRIENDS

COMMENTS I CAN SAY TO MY FRIENDS:

1.

2.

3.

QUESTIONS I CAN ASK MY FRIENDS:

1.

2.

3.

COMPLIMENTS I CAN GIVE MY FRIENDS:

1.

2.

3.

WHY????? DO WE DO THESE things WHEN WE TALK TO OTHERS???

1.

2.

3.

Name_____ Date_____

CREATING A CONVERSATION
Which means it goes both ways!!!
...and the other person does not know what you are about to do!

Think about the other person...what do you know about them?

1. _____
2. _____
3. _____

Think of the other person...how do they feel today? What do they like to talk about?

1. _____
2. _____
3. _____

Think of 3 things you want to ask the other person about themselves.

1. _____
2. _____
3. _____

Think of 3 things you want to tell the other person about yourself.

1. _____
2. _____
3. _____

Go for it; start the conversation and see if you can ask and tell your 6 items.

Name_____   Date_____

ONCE WE HAVE A FRIEND, WE KEEP FRIENDLY FILES IN OUR HEAD....

As we get to know someone, we learn information about them from small talk, conversations and observations of what they like. We store this information in a file in our brain. When we see person again, we "look in that file" to review what we know about them. Then we ask them related questions.

Think of someone you are friends with or think about what you know about someone in your present group and write 3 questions you could ask that person.

1.

2.

3.

Why do we keep asking questions of someone we already know?

Now we are going to practice, with the focus being on how many FOLLOW-UP questions you can ask them, so that you can learn more information to put into your file.

Name _____ Date _____

REVIEWING TYPES OF CONVERSATIONS...

Getting to know people starts with a SOCIAL CONVERSATION...

1. Looking at the person to see how he feels, what he is interested in, etc.
2. Greetings
3. Small talk

    Small talk is a quick exchange of questions and answers that covers a range of topics. Use the information from small talk to learn about the other person.

4. Conversation

    This is when you converse on one topic over an extended period of time where you take turns questioning, answering and commenting about the topic. This is when you get to learn more specific information about a person.

What is the purpose of this type of conversation???

_____

A FORMAL CONVERSATION is a conversation with a direct purpose. This is the type of conversation you have with a teacher, boss or when you want money from your parents!

1. Start with looking...to see how someone feels, if they are busy, if they are interested.

2. Greetings

Page 2: Reviewing types of conversations...

3. Conversation that is driven by a specific topic announced at the start of the discussion: "I want to talk to you about..."

What is the purpose of this type of conversation???

_____

How do making impressions and thinking about others fit into both of the above conversations????

_____

Just a thought...

When conversing we are told you are supposed to "tell the truth." Sometimes our opinion is true to us, but it can hurt others...

TRUTH CAN BE A TRICKY THING!

Telling the TRUTH about how you FEEL about another person, WHEN it is not going to make the other person FEEL GOOD is tricky. If you choose your wording carefully then it is called a "constructive criticism." If your wording causes the person to feel bad about them self and about you, then it just plain hurts. When you hurt someone you make a bad impression on them...and you know how that works!

4. Difficulty with Non-Verbal Communication:

The complete communication package includes the words we say as well as all the things we do while speaking and listening. Proficient use of this package is difficult. The impressions we make upon others depend on how well we succeed at this task.

Communicative success requires us to:
1. Formulate the message
2. Match non-verbal aspects of communication to the message when both speaking and listening.
3. Process the message simultaneously to consider the deeper meaning!
4. Recognize that these factors will all disappear as soon as the message is complete.

Non-verbal communication consists of:

    i.   *Body language*: This is how your body looks to the speaker. For example, if your shoulders are turned away from the group you are standing in, you are actually communicating that you do not want to be part of that group!

    ii.   *Facial expression*: These are the movements of the face that convey emotion. Many high-level students are familiar with the meanings of expressions on a person's face, but they fail to account for them or respond to them during the run of the conversation. Thus, it is essential for lessons to include not only "reading a face" but also knowing how to respond to facial expression.

iii. ***Proximity or Personal Space:*** This is how close or how far you are standing from a person. Proximity rules are dependent on culture. In the United States there is generally a "one arm rule," meaning that you are supposed to stand about the length of your arm away from another person.

iv. ***Gestures:*** These are specific movements that convey a limited set of meanings. For example, pointing with an index finger generally means to look in the direction to which the finger is pointing; a shrug of the shoulders means "I don't know."

v. ***Eye-Contact:*** This is the use of the eyes to follow the face of another person to establish and maintain communicative contact. Like facial expression, high-level students may be able to establish eye-contact, but not fully realize what it is that they are supposed to be gaining by looking at the face of another person. Teaching the concept of eye-contact needs to cover:

    A. Looking in the direction of a person's face, which is different than "staring" into their eyes

    B. While looking at them, you should be "reading their face" and interpreting the meaning of the expression

    C. Once interpreted, a response should be formulated that relates to the look on their face and the words they said

For example, a student was talking to a person, while noticing that the person looked down at their watch. The student then asked, "are you in a hurry?" That was a perfect response involved with using eye-contact to read contextual information.

77

vi. ***Volume, tone and speed of voice:*** All these components carry messages about our inner thoughts.

I often give the example of how I may speak to another person when I say, "It's nice to see you." I can say it in a pleasant voice, a teasing voice or a rude voice, with each tone of voice carrying a specific message.

Reviewing examples, and then monitoring each other in the group related to these aspects is fun. I find students learn better through personal exploration in real time interactions and related group discussion rather than role plays.

Therapeutic tools for exploring abstract and inferential language:

Normal conversation provides heaps of information from which we can explore abstract and inferential information, as does the classroom literature, history or social studies text. However, having fun with this concept is half the battle. Persons with an abstract disability and more concrete minds are not fond of having to learn about features of abstract language!

Watching sitcoms, movies or looking at advertisements in magazines can be entertaining ways to work towards increasing awareness and use of the many different features of abstract and inferential language. Below is a list of ways in which I use these mediums to explore specific concepts:

Watching movies or sitcoms as learning tools:
    a. Allows us to pause the film and <u>predict what may happen next</u>
    b. <u>Sitcoms are particularly loaded with idiomatic language, overly dramatic facial expression and socially inappropriate behaviors (this is what much of the humor is based on!).</u> The pause button is a wonderful tool for evaluating the meaning of body language. I prefer "Home Improvement" episodes. These are good for evaluating the ongoing relationships between the star (Tim Allen) and his work partner, neighbor and wife. What is the perspective of each person regarding Tim?
    c. <u>Explore problems and solutions that arise during the show.</u> Did the solution chosen solve the problem or create another one? Use the problem solving worksheet (page 16) to map out how they did it on the show.
    d. <u>Follow one specific character and monitor their emotional states across the show.</u>

Use of magazines as learning tools:
(Personal favorites for eliciting responses are *Life* and *National Geographic*.)

    a. With magazines <u>locate advertisements that are literal vs. those that are abstract.</u> The abstract advertisements do not directly appear to sell the product being advertised. Ask the group why the advertisers would choose to sell a product, such as a car, by picturing a father and son swimming in a pool. In my high-school group we evaluated a series of advertisements that sell cigarettes. It was determined that all the ads showed very attractive people relaxing in some way. What was the hidden message in the cigarette advertisements?

b. <u>Locate pictures in articles that demonstrate human emotion or interaction.</u>
   i. Label the emotion
   ii. Describe the context. Does the context contribute meaning to the picture? In one lesson I did with students a picture showed a group of firemen holding flowers near a casket. I asked the students to consider how the meaning would change if instead of a casket there was a bride.
   iii. Provide a "title" for the picture (demonstrating gestalt thinking).
   iv. If two persons are interacting in a picture, make guesses about what each would be saying to the other.
   v. Make guesses about the sequence of events; what happened before and after the picture was taken?

IDEAS FOR WRITING GOALS AND OBJECTIVES RELATED TO ABSTRACT LANGUAGE...

The following are some initial suggestions for the type of goals and objectives we may want to use when working with these students:

Goal:
Increase awareness and use of social pragmatic skills in therapy setting.

Objectives:
1. Active participation 90% of the time in a social skills group, reviewing different aspects of social communication.
2. Define what is meant by terms such as "turn-taking," "interrupting," "eye-contact," "listening," "maintaining a conversation," (etc.) with 80% accuracy.
3. Provide appropriate greeting, without a cue, when entering/exiting a room 80% of the time.
4. Complete a "creating conversation" sheet about different members of the group with 90% completion.
5. Initiate conversational questions from information written on the "creating conversation sheet" with minimal cues (75% independent).
6. With initial cues, the student will use questions to seek further information from his conversational partner about an area of interest to the partner 90% of the time.

Goal:
Increase awareness and use of skills related to abstract language and thought.

Objectives:
1. He will define the difference between figurative and literal language using idiomatic examples, with 90% accuracy.
2. He will define and use appropriately in context 5 idioms weekly.
3. He will define what it means to "infer" (take what you know and guess) with 90% accuracy.
4. He will read short passages and infer meaning with 75 % accuracy.

Summary of Chapter 5
Abstract and Inferential Language:

The non-literal aspects of language that require extra elements of interpretation can be challenging for persons with social-cognitive deficits. These can be broken into four areas:

1. Inferencing: (both verbal and non-verbal)
    Requires us to take what we know about a situation and make a guess. Social communication, classroom academics and successful employment all require a person to be actively inferencing about the world around him.
2. Abstract language
    The use of words in such a way that their literal and actual meanings can be two very different entities. Metaphors, similes, sarcasm and cultural idioms are examples of figurative language that for some students are difficult to interpret.
3. Language formulation
    The ability to organize thoughts, determine appropriate word choice and apply them grammatically in sentences to create coherent verbal thoughts or paragraphs.
4. Comprehending non-verbal aspects of communication
    Components of communication that are non-verbal but weigh significantly into deciphering the total meaning of the message including: body language, facial expression, proximity, gestures, eye-contact and volume, tone and speed of voice.

"I

LAUGH"

Chapter 6

Understanding Perspective Taking:

Thinking About Others and How They

Think About You!

The ability to begin to take the perspective of another is as fundamental as breathing to those of us who do not live with social-cognitive deficits. From an early age we conceived of the notion that others think about us and that we think about them. By reading the environmental context combined with a person's facial expression, body language, tone of voice, loudness of voice and words said one could gain quick and relatively easy access to a person's "inner thoughts."

In their book, *Mindblindness*, Baron-Cohen and Jolliffe (1997) demonstrate that mid-functioning persons with autism have impairments in the development of a Theory of Mind (ToM), which I will refer to as "perspective taking." It has been more difficult to prove empirically that persons with high-functioning autism (HFA) and Asperger Syndrome (AS) also have ToM deficits. Kazak, Collis and Lewis (1997) found that persons with autism must have higher verbal skills than their matched normal control group in order to describe attributes about themselves and others. In a recent study, Baron-Cohen and Joliffe (1997) found evidence of subtle mind reading deficits in AS adults. This AS group of subjects had difficulty inferring the mental state of persons from information in photographs of persons' eyes. The authors comment that "the results indicate that there are subtle ToM deficits in HFA and AS, at later points in development and at higher points on the I.Q. continuum than previously demonstrated; thus while this was a very advanced test of ToM, it is still far less complicated than the demands of day to day social exchanges."

Neurotypical people's easy access to this "unspoken" world of thinking and knowing is often a mystery to persons who live with social-cognitive deficits. It can also be a cause of great frustration.

Tyler, 18, was asked to consider a teacher's message and decipher what "she really meant" by saying it. Tyler grew irritated saying that "hiding information was like lying," after all, "he always said what he meant, why didn't others?"

Randy, a 16-year-old with Asperger Syndrome, had just returned from the winter holiday. I asked him how he felt to return from the vacation; he responded that he wasn't very happy to be back at school, and he'd rather still have his free time. I asked him how he thought I felt. He responded, "I have no idea!" I explained to him that most people have common reactions to global experiences. For example, if we had an earthquake we would all feel nervous, and when we go on vacation few of us really want to return to work. His response was, "no one ever told me that before!"

Not cluing in to the emotional rhythms or "hidden messages" of peers and associates can leave our students feeling like they are constantly left out. For many high-level students it appears that they may actually understand, from reading facial expressions, how someone is feeling, *but what they often do not know is how they should respond to the person.* Depression is highly linked to adolescents with this disability (Attwood, 1998). Contrary to some anecdotal reports I have read, virtually all persons with social-cognitive deficits desire friendships that are "real" and lasting. They desperately want to know how to relate to persons individually and in a group, but can't determine how they can enter into these relationships or what sets them apart. Technically they appear to have all the skills: verbally adept, creative intelligence and usually a terrific sense of humor. Their lack of "relatedness" with others (particularly unfamiliar persons) is intangible, an abstract variable that they can't begin to explore through self-discovery. Yet, it is this variable that is the invisible cloak that hangs over all persons, determining our success in social relationships.

THE FIRST STEPS TOWARDS TEACHING ABOUT PERSPECTIVE TAKING:

As educators of persons with social-cognitive deficits, one of our greatest challenges is to consider how this abstract concept of "perspective taking" can be task-analyzed into concrete and hierarchical segments from which to guide students to begin exploring this process.

GIVING THE STUDENT KNOWLEDGE:

As educators, we need to know what we are teaching and why we are teaching it! The social skills that we frequently allude to in our therapies (turn-taking, eye-contact, proximity) are all features that work to increase the "appropriateness" of behavior to make an improved "impression" upon the communicative partner. Social skills are essentially taught to help individuals make a better impression upon others. Yet, in therapy sessions, these skills are often delivered as separate units, without clear understanding to the student how each skill contributes to the greater concept of social relatedness.

Reviewed in Chapter 11, <u>Teaching So Our Teaching Sticks</u>, the initial and most important points to teaching our students are that we inform them:

1. What concept we are teaching

2. Why the concept is important

3. How the concept relates back to the larger concept of social relatedness

These lessons are the most important when providing information to students on perspective taking. Every lesson we offer and every moment of our clinical work together involves perspective taking. The steps that I work through when introducing and maintaining this concept across therapy sessions are outlined below. Beyond this outline, more specific information about teaching some of the concepts will be reviewed.

1. Introduce "perspective taking" at the very beginning of the group work so that it can be explored across each session. We can introduce it using simpler language that works for persons of all ages, such as "thinking about others, and how they think about you."

2. "Thinking about how people think" involves exploring how we make impressions (Social Skill Strategies, 1989):
    a.   By how you LOOK.
    b.   By what you SAY.
    c.   By what you DO.

3. As students get the concepts involved with "making impressions" we then explore more deeply a variety of aspects related to forming a perspective about a person. Through a process of brainstorming with a team of clinicians, we have so far "discovered" these characteristics of perspective taking:

    a.   Perspective taking has MEMORY. What do you remember about this person, and your last interaction with them?
    b.   Perspective taking requires an "immediate read" of the person. This is the time we "make impressions" upon others, and form impressions about the persons we are talking to.
    c.   Perspective taking requires us to consider the past and present emotions of persons.
    d.   Perspective taking requires us to ANALYZE all the above information.
    e.   Perspective taking requires us to RESPOND to the above information.
    f.   Active perspective taking requires us to do all of the above with a fair degree of immediacy.
    g.   On-going perspective taking happens when we consider our interaction *after we have completed*

it, and have more thoroughly considered the impression we made upon the person. At this point we may choose to call the person to clarify possible misinterpretations that could have occurred during the interaction.

4. For students in high school or above we will review and further explore the complexity of perspective taking, starting with:

   a. I see you and think about you (read the impressions you are giving me).
   b. You see me and think about me (you read the impressions I am giving you).
   c. As we talk, I think of your perspective of me and adjust my behavior accordingly, to continue to have you think about me the way I want you to.
   d. As we talk, you think of my perspective of you and you adjust your behavior accordingly, to continue to have you think about me the way I want you to.

MAKING IMPRESSIONS:

As mentioned above, teaching students that they make impressions upon others whenever they are around people is the first lesson. Many persons with social-cognitive deficits believe that they make impressions only during really significant moments in their day or life. When asked when they make impressions, typical responses include: "at the doctor's office," "at a job interview," "when my teacher was grading my paper." Thus, the concept that people form ideas about them by merely being in their presence is something most students have not considered.

Sam was a high school student who felt unable to be part of social groups at lunch. We discussed the concept of "making impressions" as something that is unavoidable at school, regardless of the time of day. Something as simple as greeting classmates in the hall between classes can affect who will want to hang out with you later in the day. Sam described that when the bell rang to go to the next class, he would quickly charge through the halls with his head down, not acknowledging anyone. We discussed how people would fail to consider him as a "friend" if he constantly passed familiar peers without acknowledging them. His homework was to slow down, keep his head up and say "hi" to at least two peers during each transitional break in his day as an initial step before seeking those peers out to have lunch with.

I have a poster on the wall in my therapy room which describes the impression making process:

YOU MAKE IMPRESSIONS BY....

1. How you look....
   a. Hygiene
   b. Clothes you wear, hairstyle

2. By what you say....
   a. Just the words you use

3. By what you do....
   a. Body language & gestures
   b. Facial expression
   c. Tone of voice
   d. Proximity
   e. Loudness, pitch of voice, etc.

A. HOW YOU LOOK:

This refers specifically to the clothes you wear, your hairstyle and hygiene. We play with the idea that clothes are costumes that change with the different settings. When introducing the concept I ask the kids how they would feel if they came for their therapy session and I was waiting for them in my wedding dress.

It is difficult for some of our students to adapt their clothing to the different seasons. They ask questions such as: "How do you know when to switch from long sleeves to short sleeves?" Some have sensory issues related to clothing preferences. It is not expected that by simply discussing this that students will change their clothing choices. However, understanding that their clothing sends a message is important. Discussing hairstyle and hair colors (e.g. dreadlocks, blue hair...) gives a chance to explore how hair choices can influence others' impressions of you. The overall purpose is to help students be aware of the factors by which other people may be forming opinions about them.

Finally, hygiene is especially important to address for young adolescents entering puberty. At times it is important to go into specific detail about how a person perceives another person who is not clean, and what impression that makes.

Todd was a high school student with constantly dirty hair. I had worked with Todd and his father for a year trying to get Todd to "clean up his act." After a year of very little change, I thought to ask Todd if he understood how I knew that his hair was dirty. He responded that he did not. We went to the nurse's bathroom and looked at our heads. I showed him how my hair looked "perky." He noted how his hair looked wet. I explained about that being what we call "greasy hair." Given those concrete descriptors, Todd did a better (not perfect!) job of keeping his hair clean.

For some students, hygiene becomes a big issue as students and teachers may notice poor cleanliness and want to help remedy the situation. I worked with a set of twin boys who needed to be taken through each step of expected cleanliness and create a hygiene maintenance schedule, to be applied at home, before they could modify their patterns. Remarkably, the time spent on this was well worth it, as they started to shower and wash clothing regularly. The only glitch was how often to wash their jackets? We never really sorted out the frequency for that, thus odor continued to be carried to school, in spite of body cleanliness!

B. BY WHAT YOU SAY:

High-level students with social-cognitive deficits are often *extremely* verbal. Many of our students believe that the communicative weight of a message is fully dependent on the specific words chosen to say it. I introduce this lesson by having students look at a continuum from 0-100% and ask them to mark what percentage of the communication is based on *"the words we say"* and what percentage is based on *"what we do"* when we are communicating. After a group discussion, I diagram that generally *20-40% of our message is communicated by the words spoken, and the other 60-80% is communicated by what we do while speaking.*

The communication connection

20-40% of
the total message
is related to the
specific words said.

60-80% of the total message relates to what we do with our body when communicating.

The one time these percentage type rules don't hold true is when someone swears or says something startling (e.g. Mrs. Winner, you look really old!). Reviewing how words impact or fail to impact communication is a good lesson. Throughout sessions, be on the lookout for words that carry too much meaning (usually these are said inappropriately!) or words that are buried by what the person is doing at the time he said them. When, during the group, a message is spoken that stands out, stop the group and ask what type of impression those words made… Allow the group time to explore meanings and interpretations!

C. BY WHAT YOU DO:

As mentioned above, what we do when speaking generally carries a lot more communicative weight than exactly how we say it. Message meaning can be modified through any or all of the following concepts:

1. Body language & gestures
2. Proximity or personal space
3. Facial expression
4. Eye-contact
5. Speed, tone and volume of voice

Each of these components is described in detail in Chapter 5 on abstract and inferential language. As mentioned previously, stopping group sessions to review how a person's use of these components affected the meaning of a message, for good or bad, is appropriate towards teaching their true value in the communicative setting.

Once all aspects of "making impressions" are thoroughly explored they can and should be used across every session. I give my older students (middle school and above) "impression awards" at the completion of a session when the group votes on who made the best impression in each of the three categories (e.g. How you look, what you say and what you do). This gives us a chance to reflect on the perspectives formed in the group that day based on a student's ability to relate across these 3 areas. If a student was really disruptive to the group that day, their behavior is also discussed in the context of these 3 components.

We also focus on creating group experiences that require a student to consider the needs of another. In a summer program, each student was responsible for making the lunch for another student. This required the sandwich-maker to interview the sandwich-eater regarding personal likes/dislikes. It also required the sandwich-maker to consider how a meal should look so as to impress (or at least not gross-out) the sandwich-eater. While this sounds like a simple experience it was one that helped students to "stop and think" about social rules related to food handling and presentation in a way none of them had considered before!

It is worth repeating... that until students understand how the specific social skills being taught relate back to the big picture of making impressions/perspective taking, it will be difficult to achieve meaningful carryover outside of the therapy setting!

Beyond Impression Making...

Perspective-taking begins with the understanding that we form internal representations of people that we carry with us, long after a communicative interaction is complete. While "making impressions" has an initial and ongoing impact, it is more involved than the surface structure presented above. As I have focused my work on teaching aspects of perspective taking I learned that beyond our first meeting with a person, perspective taking relies heavily on memory!

Bob was a 13-year-old who was part of a middle school group consisting of 2 other students. He came to the group complaining that when I left the room to talk to all the parents at the end of the sessions, Josh would call him names. I was disturbed to hear this and spoke to the entire group at the beginning of the next session to explain how the concepts of respect and perspective taking that we had discussed during the group needed to continue when the group ended for the day! Josh apologized, promising it would not happen again. About 10 minutes later during that session, Bob called Josh a "fetus" out of the blue. I stopped what we were doing and concentrated on that statement. Bob pointed out that it was not a "bad word." So we discussed what a "fetus" is (a child still in the embryo that was helpless) and I asked Josh if he liked being called that. Josh replied, "NO!" It was also noted that Bob frequently called people names during our weekly sessions. I pointed out that Josh, who had gotten in trouble by me at the start of the session, knew to wait until I was out of the room to call another student a name, but Bob called students names regardless of whether I was present or not. Bob responded to that statement by saying, "Isn't that interesting!" We then went on to discuss how "perspective taking has memory." Bob may call Josh a name at one moment thinking it is funny; however, Josh holds onto the moment only to retaliate later. We compared this to school when a student insults a peer to get a laugh early in the day, and then that peer shuns him later in the day.

Carol Gray, in her book, *Comic Strip Conversations* (1994) illustrates how we revise our messages according to how they will affect the listener. On the next page I take this one step further and illustrate how we make that revision.

THINKING AND SAYING....
ARE TWO DIFFERENT THINGS!

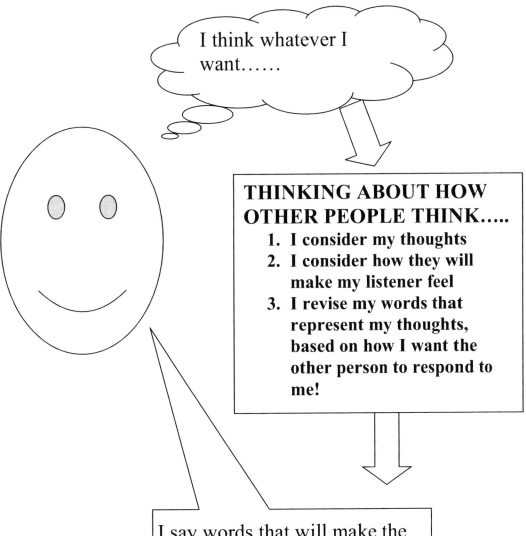

I think whatever I want......

THINKING ABOUT HOW OTHER PEOPLE THINK.....
1. **I consider my thoughts**
2. **I consider how they will make my listener feel**
3. **I revise my words that represent my thoughts, based on how I want the other person to respond to me!**

I say words that will make the effect I want to make on my listener: If I want to make the person feel good, I choose words to do that. I can also choose words that can hurt someone, if I want to do that. *The problem comes when I say words that are unexpected or that hurt someone when I don't mean to.*

Perspective taking is a very active process that requires an individual to constantly ***observe, analyze and respond*** to the changing dynamics of the person they are interacting with. Shifting through this ongoing continuum is not easy for persons with social-cognitive deficits (or for any of us at times!), but time in the group is well spent evaluating this process and the corresponding product, *how another individual thinks of you.*

The use of worksheets on perspective taking in group sessions:

The following is a series of worksheets developed to help teach this process. As we are in the infancy of developing this program, use your own creativity to keep expanding upon it. If you feel you have hit upon a new important theme, please let me know!
Worksheets relate to:

- ❑ Impression making
- ❑ Social relationships
- ❑ Communicative expectations
- ❑ Complexities of perspective taking

Worksheets are used to help guide discussions, not as an end to themselves! A down-side to group discussion is that one or two students can dominate, without the leader getting a clear idea of how the other group participants are understanding the information. Since we know that visually based teaching helps focus attention, I almost always have a written lesson paired with a discussion so that the students can demonstrate how they have processed the information on their own.

Worksheets on "Making Impressions" are on pages 102-104.

Name_____ Date_____

MAKING IMPRESSIONS...

What are the components of each of these 3 areas?

1. By how you look...

    a._____

    b._____

2. By what you say...

    a._____

3. By what you do...

    a._____

    b. _____

    c. _____

    d._____

Name_____ **Date**_____

The 3 ways in which someone will think about you and you about them (making impressions)

1. By how they/you look
2. By what they/you say
3. By what they/you do

Explore:

- How can you adjust your behavior if you start to think they are not thinking well of you?

  _____

- Describe ways that you can adjust "what you say."_____
- Describe ways you can adjust "what you do."

  _____

- Describe ways you can comment on how a person looks._____

Continued Perspective Taking:

Involves using your memory of the last communicative exchange you had with another person, and determining further how it should be interpreted.

Explore (things to think about):
- How did the communication go overall?
- What is that person's lasting impression of me now that the communication is complete? What is my perspective of that person?
- What do I think of them now that the communication is complete?
- Next time I see that person what will he expect from me?

Name_____ Date_____

IMPRESSIONS FOR A JOB INTERVIEW

- BY WHAT YOU DO:
    - Facial expression
    - Eye contact
    - Attention to interviewer
    - Gestures
    - Posture in your chair
    - Staying on the topic
    - Tone of voice

- BY WHAT YOU SAY:
    - The words you use.
    - Put a positive spin on events (I can, I will, etc... rather than I can't)
    - Be prepared for questions like: What are 3 strengths and weaknesses..?

- BY HOW YOU LOOK:
    - The clothes you wear
    - Your hygiene
    - Your hair style

I will prepare for a job interview by doing the following:

_____
_____
_____
_____
_____

The following pages are worksheets related to understanding social relationships and communicative expectations. The later worksheets are intended for younger elementary school-aged students. All others are intended for middle-school-aged students and above.

At times we educators use terms such as "Social Relationships" without clearly defining what they mean. The first two worksheets are an attempt to define the term "social relationships."

Communicative expectations relate to perspective taking. Understanding what people expect from us, and what we expect from them in communicative settings helps to demystify the communicative process. When expectations are not met or behavior is significantly different than what is expected, odd impressions are formed. These worksheets are provided as a start towards fostering thoughts and discussions around these various topics.

Name_____ Date_____

WHAT IS A SOCIAL RELATIONSHIP????

Now that we are getting older, people use bigger words…. In our group we work on understanding social relationships, but what does that mean?

What does social mean?_____

What does "relationship" mean?_____

Describe a good social relationship you have or have had:

_____
_____
_____
_____
_____

What makes or made it good?

_____
_____
_____
_____
_____

Name_____Date_____

THINKING ABOUT OTHERS WHO LIVE IN MY HOME:

Thinking about others includes thinking about people I live with. As I get older, I have more responsibility to the people I live with.

Household responsibilities I have include:

1.

2.

3.

These are things I know I should do to help. When I was younger I needed to be reminded a lot to do these things. Now that I am older it is expected that I should have to be told _____times before I do them. However, usually I have to be told _____ times before I do them!

When my parents have to tell me what they expect from me over and over again, I feel:

_____.

My parents also have feelings about this; they feel_____.

Page 2: Thinking About Others Who Live In My House

I also have responsibilities to the social relationships I have in my house. I will define that as meaning:

_____

_____

_____

_____

Here are the people that live in my house, and their particular interests:

1.

2.

3.

4.

Social relationships start with thinking about how the other person thinks. This is called Taking Their
_____. Commenting, questioning and complimenting <u>while acting like I am serious about my words</u> (for example: not being sarcastic), are all parts of what develops healthier social relationships. Healthy social relationships are important towards growing up because they help me to learn about

_____

_____

Page 3: Thinking About Others Who Live In My House

I can develop more mature social relationships by using the above information and then doing the following with:
My mom:

My dad:

My sibling:

Name _____ **Date**_____

People think, I think, you think, they think…..

What are the differences?????

Different types of people expect different things from you, and you expect different behavior from different types of people as well.

What do you expect from….

TEACHERS	FRIENDS	PARENTS

What do they expect from you????

TEACHERS	FRIENDS	PARENTS

Page 2 (People think....)

Would a teacher from school expect a different set of behaviors from you if you saw her at a holiday party that is not held at school? Yes____ No____

What behaviors would she now expect from you that are different from when she sees you in school?

_____

_____

What behaviors would she expect to stay the same?

_____

_____

WHY???????_____

_____

Name _____ *Date*_____

WHAT DO PEOPLE EXPECT???

They expect me to:
1. Behave...what does that mean?

2. Communicate...what does that mean?

How I am expected to behave and communicate changes in different places or settings...

What do people expect from me:

1. In the classroom?

2. At recess?

3. At home when at the dinner table?

4. At home when playing?

5. At home when it is bedtime?

6. Visiting someone's office?

How do people feel if I behave and talk the way they expect me to?

How do people feel if I behave and talk in a way that is surprising (unexpected) to them?

Name_____ Date_____

I THINK, YOU THINK

Why do you like to have friends?

1.

2.

Why does your friend like to be friends with you?
What is special about you?

1.

2.

What does your friend want you to do for him?
Friends have feelings too, how can you make
him/her feel good?

1.

2.

Friends have to do stuff for EACH OTHER!

Name one really important thing you can do for
your friend:

This next set of worksheets was developed to help set some ground rules for working together as a group. While persons with social-cognitive deficits are generally fun, warm people, their lack of perspective taking can make it difficult at times to work with them in a group!! This worksheet went a long way in helping students understand the needs of each participant, including me, the teacher!

Name_____ Date_____

Groups of people...
Groups of needs....

What are the needs of the members of this group?

1. Your needs?

2. Needs of other students in the group?

3. The teacher's needs?

If we aren't meeting the needs of all the folks in the group, then we have a problem. Problems need to be solved and we will have to take the time to fill out a problem solving worksheet and then follow through on it. Fair? ...I think so!

SOLVING PROBLEMS BEFORE THEY BECOME PROBLEMS

1. **What is the problem?**

_____

2. **What choices do you have to solve the problem?**

1. a bad choice:	**2.** a good choice:	**3.** a good choice:

3. **Write in possible consequences of each choice:**

1.	**2.**	**3.**

1. **What choice or choices are best to pick?**_____

2. **When are you going to start to solve your problem? (List time and/or date)**_____

3. **Where are you going to do this? (Location)**

_____

4. **Who do you need to talk to, to help? (Person)**

_____

5. **What are you going to say or ask?**

_____
_____

NOTES

The next worksheet was developed for a group of middle-school aged boys I was working with. It came from a discussion we had one day about the boys never letting anyone see the real them. What they did let people see was their "dark side." After completing the worksheet, one of the boys with more difficult behaviors in the group commented, "There really is a nice person inside of me! Sometimes when I am with friends I wish I could just tell them that the inside of me is really good!" This worksheet allowed the group the opportunity to discuss who they really are and how their communicative behaviors often keep them from letting people see the "shining side" of their personality.

Name_____ Date_____

LETTING PEOPLE IN TO SEE
THE REAL ME!

We all have at least 2 sides to our personality....

List 3 ways that you show people your "Dark Side" (this is the meaner side of you).

1.

2.

3.

List 3 ways that you can show people your "Shining Side" (this is the nicer side of you).

1.

2.

3.

When do you feel like you can let people INSIDE??

This final set of worksheets is for older high school students and young adults.

Name _____ Date_____

The Complexities of Perspective Taking...

Immediate perspective taking starts with the immediate situation when you first see someone. But then it continues in memory to be interpreted further at a later time. We will call this "Continued perspective taking."

<u>Immediate perspective taking:</u>

Immediate Perspective Taking progresses at least 4 ways...

1. **You think about the other person as soon as you see them.**

2. **The other person thinks about you as soon as they see you.**

3. **You think about what the other person is thinking about you....and you adjust your behavior accordingly to how you want them to perceive you.**

4. **The other person thinks about what you think about them...and they adjust their behavior accordingly to how they want you to perceive them.**

Page 2: The complexities of Perspective Taking

Explore:

❑ **What does that person expect from you to begin with?**

List 4 behaviors people would expect from you when communicating with them:

_____

_____

❑ **How do different situations change what people expect from you when you are conversing?**

At school or a job:

_____

With a friend:

_____

At home:

_____

❑ **How do you begin to "guess" what they might be thinking about you? What signs do you look for?**

_____

_____

_____

❑ **How do you really know if your guess is right?**

_____

❑ **Do you always know?** _____

❑ **Why do you adjust your behavior?**

_____

Name _____ Date_____ :

Gaining Perspective on Our Behaviors at Home....

Interview your sibling to find out his/her perspective about you:

1. What are things you do in the community that embarrasses him/her?

2. If you were to work on one of these things, which is the one that bothers him/her the most?

Your perspective on your sibling:

There are things that your sibling does that you do not like either. Write down what you wish your sister/brother would change about her/himself.

If he/she was to work on one of these things, which one would you like her/him to work on?

Name_____ Date_____

A FOCUS ON PERSPECTIVE: YOURS AND OTHERS'

Conversations are about making good impressions and remembering to take the other person's perspective while sharing information. Many social conversations are really not about exchanging facts as much as they are about learning to "relate to" and "understand" the other person.

In conversations you have to deal with two aspects:

1. The verbal message of language

2. The non-verbal message of body language. The things you do with your body when you talk to another person are more important than the things you do with your words!!! Eye-contact is part of body language.

List 3 other ways you communicate with body language:

1.

2.

3.

Homework:

Interview 1 person in your family to find out their perspective about how it is to talk to you.

Page 2   A focus on perspective....
INTERVIEW #1

Am I easy to talk to? Why?

What are some good conversational strategies I use?

What could I do better that would make it easier for you to have a conversation with me?

...Then evaluate what your perspective was when talking to them.

Were they easy to talk to? Why?

What were some good conversational strategies they used?

What could they have done better in the conversation?

IDEAS ON GOALS AND OBJECTIVES FOR INITIAL STUDY OF PERSPECTIVE TAKING

Goal:
Increase awareness and use of skills related to understanding own and other's perspective.

> **Objectives:**
> 1. The student will list 3 ways he/she makes an impression, explaining what each means with 90% accuracy.
> 2. Maintain a perspective journal where the student records 3 good and 3 bad impressions he made about himself or someone else during the week, with 90% consistency.
> 3. While participating in the group, the student will self-monitor the impression he/she is making (or self-monitor the impression others are giving) with 75% accuracy.
> 4. When participating in the conversational group, he will be able to accurately "guess" the emotional state of the different members at the table over the course of the session with 75% accuracy.
> 5. When talking about personal events in the student's daily life he will use at least 3 different emotional terms to describe his reaction/perspective of the events.
> 6. He will describe his speech and language goals with 90% accuracy.
> 7. He will describe what behaviors he needs to modify to meet his goals, using the concepts of self-awareness, self-control and self-monitoring with 90% accuracy.

Summary: Chapter 6, Understanding Perspective Taking

Considering the needs and thoughts of others, as well as one's own, is what I am referring to as perspective taking. Persons with social-cognitive deficits are limited in their ability (when compared to what's expected with their IQ) to think about others, and how others are thinking about them. Relatively little work has been done to guide us on how to teach this subject to our students. My thought on this is to start by teaching that we all make impressions based on:

1. How we look
2. What we say
3. What we do

A series of worksheets and strategies are introduced in this chapter to foster our thinking on the process of teaching this highly complicated and normally intuitive process in a more concrete manner. Facilitating discussions about this concept in group sessions with older students is ideal for increasing awareness of others and our own thoughts.

"I LAUGH"

Chapter 7

Getting the Big Picture:

Gestalt Processing

We are constantly alert to information around us. We then sort through it, pick out the most salient features and discard the rest. Through this process we are able to focus on what is relevant, follow underlying themes, and generally make logical sense out of all that goes before us. Neurotypical folks do this intuitively. Our students have great difficulty filtering the information they absorb and pulling it together in a meaningful way. Even for very bright persons with this disability, making sense of their environment can be overwhelming at best. This difficulty is referred to in the literature as the "Central Coherence Theory" (Frith, 1989).

Deficits related to not understanding the gestalt can have a significant impact on the learning process. However, these deficits are not easy to observe or quantify through testing, making it difficult to acknowledge their existence.

When gestalt-processing abilities are not at the same level as overall academic intellectual functioning:

1. **Knowledge is learned in islands without bridges to connect it to other knowledge. Our students often don't see the whole picture.**

   It is part of the DSM IV (1994) diagnostic criteria for both Autism and Asperger Syndrome that persons with this disability have an "encompassing preoccupation." We often see folks with social-cognitive deficits as having an extraordinary ability to concentrate on and absorb a myriad of details related to a specific topic. We also see that in the world of academics these students can often quickly learn the more factually based knowledge around certain topics of interest, amazing their school peers with their depth of information. This type of more rote intelligence can be confusing to those who relate to these people on a daily basis since on one hand they seem so "knowledgeable", but on the other hand they seem so "clueless" about bridging an island of knowledge to related islands of knowledge.

   John was a senior in high school. I had him working on activities related to understanding the gestalt. I asked him to read some "cause-effect" scenarios. One of them was about a girl who notices that all the pollywogs disappear come summer and she postulates to her father that this is because the hot sun killed them. It was John's job to determine whether her theory about the pollywogs was correct. ***John initially concluded*** *that her theory was correct. John had been in mainstreamed science classes. I asked him what he knew about pollywogs and he told me that they turn into frogs. I then asked him what he knew about seasonal mating habits of animals and he was able to describe that many animals are born in the spring. At this point he made the connection: the pollywogs did not die they simply matured into frogs.* **I explained to examine information we need to take what we know from different pools of knowledge and bind them together to make fuller conclusions.** *He liked this concept, and came back to the session the next week and was able to review the above idea about integrating information; however he again produced an error in pulling together his thinking on the next scenario that was reviewed.*

Alex was a bright senior in high school, who had just been accepted to many major universities. He had recently received his driver's license and was complaining about having to drive in all the rainy weather, explaining that his windshield wipers didn't work so he drove with his head out the window. When I asked how he knew the wipers didn't work, he confessed that he actually did not know how to turn them on, nor had he realized he should explore his dashboard. At this point I offered to escort him to his car to help him figure out how to do it, but he replied he would now explore it on his own.

The lessons for caregivers from the above scenarios are plentiful:

1. We need to teach students how to "connect knowledge" to create a greater whole.

2. We need to understand that our students, who have high verbal skills, can repeat and embellish upon what we say without beginning to process what we mean by saying it.

3. We need to give our students plenty of practical examples to explore this concept of connecting knowledge. The more we can relate the examples to their own experiences, the better.

4. We need to provide information that is clearly stated, actively encouraging our students to determine relationships and connections. Providing tools that help to analyze relationships, such as Venn diagrams and mapping of concepts is very helpful.

2. Our students often don't account for contextual cues and clues:

In the same way that they don't connect information in their brains, they have difficulty connecting what they see with their eyes. This is the classic, "They don't see the forest for the trees."

So much of how we function in real time depends on the context in which a message is stated. For example, when standing in a train station a person may ask you, "when do you think it's coming?" This is a vague question unless you consider the context of waiting for the train, in which case the question seems quite clear. Often persons with deficits in social-cognition do not interpret the meaning offered by the context.

Sam was a 9-year-old boy who was in my home for an assessment of social-cognitive functioning. We were sitting in my family room and I asked him to look at the objects in one corner of the room and determine what musical instruments my husband played, pointing out this was his hobby corner. Sam's first response was, "how will I do that?" Sam then got out of his chair and went and touched the entire set of little trombone figurines that stood on top of the piano. He then concluded that my husband must play trombone. "Very good" I responded, now what other instrument does he play?" Sam looked perplexed while he leaned on the piano (the cover was down covering the keys). After looking around for a bit he asked if we could play "hot and cold," which we did without him successfully guessing the second instrument. He finally said, "I give up, tell me." When I told him it was the piano he couldn't believe he missed "seeing" it. I gave Sam a set of 4x4" picture cards from which he was to make conclusions about "cause and effect," a task not identical, but similar to the one we had done above. I figured since the task of making guesses in the real context was tough, he would do even worse on the pictured task, but the reverse was true! He flew through the cause-and-effect pictures getting 100% accuracy.

The above example again made me stop and think: **How could there be such a discrepancy in performance between pictured and real information?** Then I realized that the pictures package the contextual information very neatly helping the student to focus and draw conclusions. Processing information in real time and space does not allow information to "jump out at you." This particular child was having difficulty qualifying for services in school. Why? Because the majority of our standardized tests use tasks such as the pictures discussed above. Virtually none of our tests explore how a child functions in his real world.

Other examples of students not understanding the big picture:

1. *When each student in a group of high school boys with high-functioning autism was asked what a particular movie was about, each responded by indicating that they **never** know what a movie is*

about!   However they could recite many details and even dialogue from the movies!

2. *When a teacher referred to different parts of an assignment, the student plugged into these individual parts without realizing that all of them fit into one global task.*

3. *When a parent wrote a sequence of how to "take a shower," her 8-year-old was observed standing in the shower holding a bottle of shampoo but not doing anything with it. When she looked at her written sequence the mother noted that she wrote "shampoo" rather than what to do with the shampoo! Since this child was not recognizing how this piece of the task fit into the whole task, he missed the concept all together.*

4. *When a student was asked to compare the similarities and differences between the Vietnam war and the Korean war, he was at a loss. He could recite many details related to each war but failed to establish that a relationship existed between them.*

5. *When a student got a job working at a local department store, he nearly lost his job because he failed to realize that determining the transportation to and from his job was an essential component to keeping a job.*

How does problem solving relate to gestalt processing?

An 11-year-old boy explained that he had a hole in his pants at school that day and was really embarrassed by the kids teasing him. He had changed his pants when he got home, after school. When a therapist asked how he fixed the problem he stated (very literally) he could not because he did not have thread at home. When she tried to have him think through his whole day and state in general what his problem was at school that day, he drew a blank and could not tell us.

The above example demonstrates how understanding the gestalt is essential for problem solving. The first task we do when we need to solve a problem is *consider what the problem is*. This requires us to look at every angle of the situation in which the problem occurred or may occur and pull out the most salient features to determine what the problem actually is. In the above case, the boy was stuck on the fact that they did not have thread to fix the pants when the actual problem was that the boy was upset that kids were teasing him *because* of the hole in his pants. If the boy were to focus on the problem being that he needed to repair the hole, he would indeed need thread. If the boy saw that the real problem was that kids were teasing him, then simply putting on a different pair of pants would actually solve the problem. Demonstrated below is how defining a problem with a gestalt understanding is important to the next step, which is making choices towards solving the problem. ***Being able to accurately isolate the real problem is essential towards effective problem solving and is probably the most difficult aspect of the entire problem solving process.***

Problem Solving: Example of how recognizing different "Problems" changes the possible solutions

Illustrated below is how one scenario, having torn pants in school, can be seen as different problems requiring different solutions depending on the stated problem (gestalt processing).
Our student who tends to look at the small details evaluated and attempted to solve the problem as in example #1, whereas a person with a larger focus to the context may define and solve it as in example #2.
Our student continued to wear his pants as-is until he got home, when his mother informed him that he should change his pants.

Example #1: What is the problem?

My pants have a hole in them.

What choices do you have to solve the problem?

1. The bad choice: Continue to wear the pants.	**2.** A good choice: Sew up the hole.	**3.** A good choice: Patch the hole.

Example #2: What is the problem?
Students are teasing me because I have a hole in my pants.

What choices do you have to solve the problem?

1. The bad choice: Continue to wear the pants.	**2.** A good choice: Call mom and have her bring me a hole-less pair of pants.	**3.** A good choice: Wear a sweatshirt that hangs down and covers the seat of my pants.

Use of facilitating frameworks (FF) to guide a student through written assignments:

A common classroom assignment of requiring students to pull their thoughts together and write them onto a lined piece of paper is often near torture to students with social-cognition deficits. Why? We know that a majority of these students have difficulty with the fine motor elements of writing. Their writing is often excessively slow and imprecise. In school, it is expected that children become fairly fluid writers by the time they are in 3rd grade. However, many of our students are still finding the process quite laborious all the way up into their older years of school. With the motoric and visual perceptual demands of the written task, our students also need to add integrated thinking on top of it all! Yikes!

Gestalt-process thinking is the heavy burden of the writing assignment. Students need to take all that they know and pull out the more salient aspects in a coherent and organized manner. For our students, mental paralysis is often the consequence of these assignments! One strategy that helps our students work through the writing process more effectively is taking a teacher's general assignment and breaking it down into a set of facilitating questions to guide the student's thinking.

For example:

I observed a 3rd grader who was supposed to write a journal entry on what he did for Thanksgiving. The teacher mentioned that he should talk about the food as well as what was fun on that day. She wrote this on the board so the student had a visual cue about the assignment, yet he sat for 10 minutes without doing anything related to the assignment. The teacher had reported that journal writing was consistently the worst part of his day.

I went over to the student and wrote 4 questions on his journal page:
1. Where did you have your Thanksgiving dinner?
2. Name 4 things you ate.
3. Who joined you for dinner?
4. What was the most fun about the day?

I left plenty of space between each question. Upon seeing the more specific questions, the student began to write the answers. He had a few minutes of inattention after completing the first two questions but was easily re-directed back to the paper to complete the last two questions. While we did not yet have a written paragraph, we did have information now that we could use to help teach about the organization and production of a paragraph. After that success, we coordinated with the resource teacher for her to work with this student twice a week to take his journal entries and help him turn the answers into paragraphs. The alternative was for him to continue with the more global assignment and literally "space out" for 20 minutes, leaving the teacher to be unhappy about his work and the student feeling unaccomplished.

While having students produce answers to more specific questions may not be the paragraph end-product that was immediately desired, at least it provides something to work with! It also gives the student the ability to complete the work rather than give him opportunities to "space out" or feel bad that he can't keep up. This process of breaking down a general assignment into more coherent parts is what I call creating a "Facilitating Framework."

Example 2:

I worked with a group of high school boys with various diagnoses, all related to social-cognitive deficits. We were planning a trip into the community. No student had the skills to anticipate the set of events that needed to be considered to make that trip possible. The students were provided a set of facilitating frameworks we called "planning sheets." The first sheet was a "decision making sheet" that provided questions that allowed each student to state his opinion about where he wanted to go on the trip and why. After negotiating as a group to go to one specific place (e.g. bowling), the next set of questions had to do with how we would get there and how much money would be needed. Each student then determined what information we didn't have, for example: How much would the bowling cost? What were the cross streets of the bowling alley? What restaurants were nearby? They then had to make a phone call to get the information. Thus, the next sheet had to do with planning phone calls and what they would say (this also involved working on initiation of communication). The activity continued until the students had worked out the details on paper and in group discussion. They were learning the PROCESS of planning and organizing through a series of guided questions. The bowling event happened successfully, but the activity was not complete. When they returned to school the next day, the final lesson was a facilitating framework that they had to fill out to review all the steps of the planning process that they had just completed. The idea of the task was to take the gestalt (going into the community), think through all the elements of organization that happened on the worksheets and in follow up discussion and then review how all the pieces fit back into the gestalt of this final review sheet after the trip.

Facilitating Frameworks are simply the idea of building an extra level of structure and organization into global assignments. They do require extra time to layout the questions (a process that is fairly easy for us neurotypical adults). However, it is time well spent since otherwise the educator or parent would most likely take time to "nag" the child to "get to work." It makes more sense to invest our time in assisting our students to "get the ball rolling."

Below is an example of a facilitating framework used with a group of high school boys who went with me to see the movie "Wild Wild West." The assignment after the movie was to write a paragraph about the movie; the questions in the framework guided their final paragraph product. The questions not only served to guide their thinking in the group discussion, but to also generate more concise responses to specific questions. After the initial questions were completed, the students wrote their short paragraphs in about 10 minutes. As you will notice we try to keep the students focused on the idea of perspective taking and problem solving as a common thread through story frameworks. Not coincidentally, these are the same skills we are also working on in their social relationships! Blending a curriculum to demonstrate how these skills generalize across different areas can only help.

Thinking about the movie "Wild Wild West"

1. What were the main problem the two main characters were trying to solve in the movie?

   _____

2. How did they solve it?

   _____

3. What was the relationship between the two men at the start of the movie?

   _____

4. What did each man think about the other at the start of the movie?

   West thought_____

   The other guy
   thought_____

5. How did this relationship cause more problems?

   _____

   _____

   _____

   _____

6. How did the differences in the two guys help to actually solve the problems?_____

_____

7. How did the relationship between the two men change by the end of the movie?

_____

_____

8. How was organization/planning important in the movie?

_____

9. Write a paragraph of at least 5 sentences, summarizing the main idea (problems encountered and perspectives taken) by people in the movie.

_____

_____

_____

_____

_____

_____

_____

Reviewed below are basic steps for creating *Facilitating Frameworks (FF)*.

The first 5 steps are all that are needed for your basic classroom assignment.

1. Visually present the framework (write it down on paper).

2. Break the lesson down into smaller component parts.

3. Facilitate active learning by writing out open-ended questions for the student to infer what is needed in each part and what the next step in the process will be.

4. Whenever possible create a temporal sequence so that the previous step needs to be completed before the next can begin.

5. Have the student work ***independently*** through the component parts once the FF structure is organized.

Along with the above, the next set of steps are used with long-term planning projects.

6. Use the student's date-book to record when specific parts of the FF are expected to be completed. This helps to incorporate the project into his standard homework routine.

7. Ask the student questions to reveal the mistakes made in the planning process, rather than directly pointing them out.

8. Employ several FF's to complete one, more complicated project. For example, when planning the trip into the community described above we used 6 FF's:

    1. To decide where to go on the trip
    2. To determine what information was needed in the community
    3. To make phone calls to get specific information
    4. To compile the overall information into a workable whole, addressing all the details
    5. To review what to do if the teacher were sick the day of the field trip
    6. To summarize the experience. For use after the field trip to help review all the steps we previously thought through to successfully plan and experience the trip

Name_____ Date_____

PROJECT PLANNING GUIDE

1. What is the project?

_____

_____

2. When is it due?_____

3. When is the rough-draft due?_____

4. If you have an outline the teacher gave you, take it out now to look at. List the contents that need to be included in the project.

_____

_____

_____

_____

5. What do I need to do to find the information (for example, internet, library, encyclopedia, etc.)? List your resources:

_____

_____

_____

_____

6. You will need to plan your project day by day. Remember, you will have other homework to do at the same time you are working on this project, so if you break the project down into smaller pieces you will be able to get all your work done without stressing out.

    a. Get out your daily calendar and write down the dates that you will collect your resources and do the research.

    a. Write down the dates when you will have written the different sections of the project so the whole project is completed by rough-draft due-date.

    b. Write in the days you will modify it to turn in for the final due date.

7. Who do you need to talk to clarify information or ask specific questions?

_____

8. When will you talk to that person? Will you need to make an appointment? When will you do that?

_____

Where will you talk to that person?

_____

Page 3 Project Planning Guide

9. What will you say?

_____

(Write down what they said, so that you can make sure you got the information right!)

10.   Now that you have followed your schedule, using your calendar every day to monitor your progress, it is now time to bring all the different sections of the project together and make a table of contents, bibliography and whatever else is needed.

11.   Look at your completed project from a different person's perspective. Does it look nice? If so, turn it in on the date it is due, or even before it is due!

Congratulations!

What does organizing and prioritizing have to do with gestalt processing?

Organization is a process through which we evaluate large bodies of information and chunk them into smaller pieces. It is virtually impossible to organize if you cannot think beyond the smaller pieces of detail. Evaluating large bodies of information is gestalt processing. However, when I ask my students if they are organized they will often reply "Yes!" because they know exactly where one of their prized possessions is kept: "My Star Trek figures are on the second shelf, next to my books." I talk to my students about "brain organization" as opposed to rigid organization of possessions. Brain organization is the ability to conceptualize groupings and then follow through with applying that concept in the environment. Whether it be organizing thoughts for a paper to write, segmenting an assignment into smaller pieces, speaking on a subject without being tangential or planning events for a holiday, organizing is crucial for academic and career success not to mention a peaceful home life.

Prioritizing:

Prioritizing can be achieved only after organizing. We have to break information into smaller chunks (organization) before we can create a hierarchy of importance (prioritization). This also requires that the student learn to recognize how one task is more or less important than another.

Thinking prior to organization:

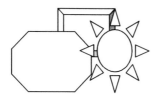

Organized thinking:

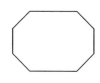

Prioritized thinking:

1.

2.

3.

Using graphic organizers to facilitate reading comprehension and written expression.

Graphic organizers are visual tools that are also referred to as "concept maps" or "mind maps". The strength of the graphic organizer is that it allows the student to visually organize information to assist with critical thinking. Wiig and Wilson (2001) describe the use of visual tools to facilitate thinking, organizing and communication. Wiig and Wilson note that the importance of visual tools is that they allow one to make visual representations of what should be information that the child understands or brainstorms internally.

Graphic organizers can take many different forms from the classic Venn diagram to contrast and compare information (see page 155 for an example), to the use of pictured representations to study a specific element of organization. For example, a picture of a train long train in which a child writes out each step of an activity or plot of a book in each car of the train.

Graphic organizers are critically important for helping students who have difficulty seeing the "forest for the trees". These visual tools help to directly teach students about the different levels of organization and related information while also helping students understand how these parts help to create the "main idea". The power of the tools is that they graphically demonstrate how concepts and details relate in hierarchies. Without the use of these tools, we expect that children can process long passages of language (written or spoken) and then can create the conceptual information in their brains as well as sort out the important from the non-essential details. Students with social cognitive deficits often have great difficulty translating language into this type of deeper meaning.

Many of our students with strong intellectual skills can easily comprehend and follow the structure of the graphic organizer and fill in the related information with minimal cues. However, students with more significant forms of social cognitive deficits may need help in understanding the basic construction and meaning of the graphic organizer. A 12-year-old boy with high functioning autism could not grasp the meaning of graphic organizers when I helped him to fill them out based on information gained from a book of literature we were reading together. Since he could not easily comprehend the meaning of the graphic organizer itself, the tool was of little help when I asked him to answer critical thinking questions related to the information we had read and which was mapped out on the paper. However, this same boy was far more successful when he was taught to create the structure of the graphic organizer and fill in the information himself. Once he grasped the meaning of the structure by learning to create it himself, he was far more able to answer critical thinking questions related to the information imbedded in the visual tool. On the next page is the organizer this student created by watching the first part of a videotaped movie. The graphic organizer was created after numerous pauses in the viewing of the movie to discuss and categorize the various details listed in the organizer. It was a difficult process for the student, but one that he clearly began to grasp by the end of the session. Due to his deficits in this area, he will continue to require consistent use of graphic organizers to help him learn how information comes together to create a conceptual structure. Without the use of this visual method, his rapid reading decoding skills lead to fairly empty reading comprehension.

Graphic organizers can have a much more defined visual structure than in the above example in that different levels of information can take on different shapes. For example, the central idea can be in a circle, the sub-ideas can be written inside squares and the related details can be encased in triangles. Most educators are familiar with the concept of the graphic organizer, which is often briefly taught in the mainstream classroom at which time it is introduced as a strategy in which students can learn to organize information usually in preparation for written expression. However, students with deficits

A graphic organizer a boy created by watching movie clips.

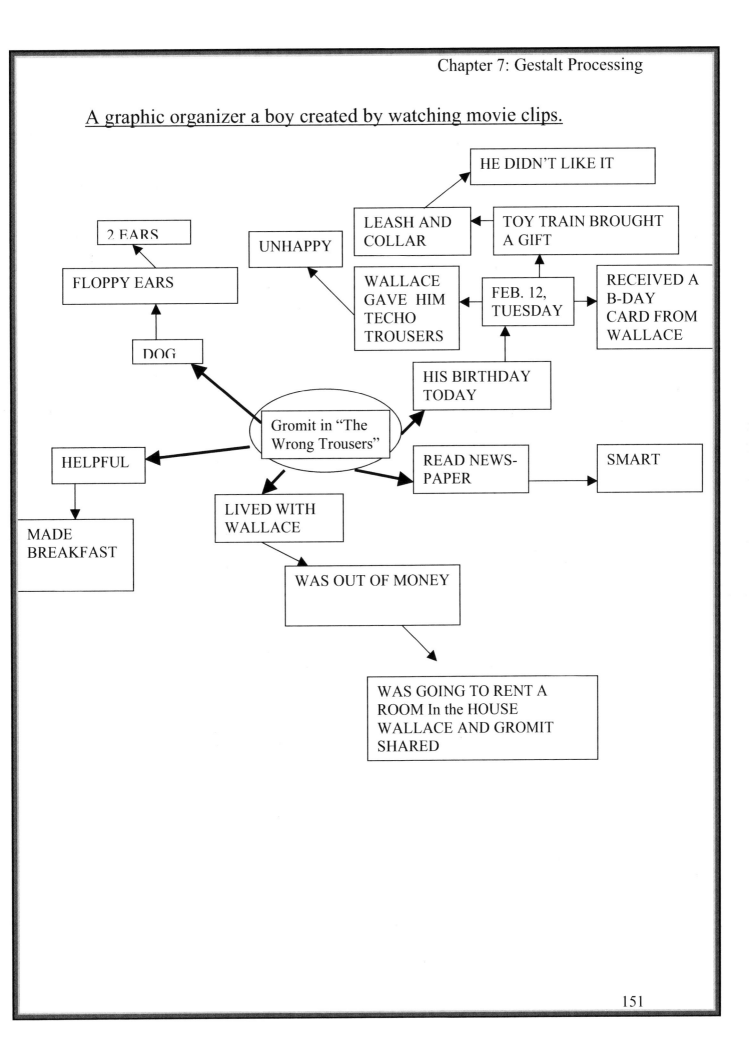

HE DIDN'T LIKE IT

LEASH AND COLLAR

TOY TRAIN BROUGHT A GIFT

2 EARS

UNHAPPY

FLOPPY EARS

WALLACE GAVE HIM TECHO TROUSERS

FEB. 12, TUESDAY

RECEIVED A B-DAY CARD FROM WALLACE

DOG

HIS BIRTHDAY TODAY

Gromit in "The Wrong Trousers"

HELPFUL

READ NEWS-PAPER

SMART

MADE BREAKFAST

LIVED WITH WALLACE

WAS OUT OF MONEY

WAS GOING TO RENT A ROOM In the HOUSE WALLACE AND GROMIT SHARED

related to understanding the gestalt need to use these types of structures intensively and over time to comprehend a wide variety of information including social structures, reading comprehension and written expression.

While typical children are encouraged to learn about graphic organizers as a way to organize information on paper or in their heads, most of our students will need to continue to need to explore this process externally by filling them out on paper. To learn more about the variety of ways graphic organizers can be structured explore books available on the topic at your local teacher's supply shop.

Some books that I have found helpful include:

- Parks, S. and Black, H. (1992) Organizing Thinking, Books 1 and 2. Critical Thinking Books and Software: Pacific Grove, CA. *These books explore how to infuse visual tools into the academic curriculum of the child across the school day.*

- Wiig, E. and Wilson, C. (2001) Map It Out. Thinking Publications, Eau Claire, WI. *This book explores a variety of ways to use visual tools to assist with comprehension of social contexts, pragmatics, reading comprehension and semantic/word meaning.*

- Flynn, K. (1995) Graphic Organizers…helping children to think visually. Creative Teaching Press, inc., Cypress, CA. *This book provides a variety of graphic organizers to use with children in elementary school. It is a simple book that is extremely useful!*

- The reader may also want to go to www.criticalthinking.com

A software program is also widely used in homes and schools to help students create graphic organizers on their computers. This program is called "Inspiration" for use with older students and "Kidspiration" for use with younger students. Both software programs can be explored at www.inspiration.com.

Even with computer software, most students continue to need assistance in creating the structure of the organizers. Even though these computer programs make the mapping neater, the process itself continues to be cognitively challenging.

Graphic organizers, as mentioned above are perhaps most commonly associated with written expression. However, from my experience the graphic organizer cannot stand alone as the only accessory to assist with the writing process. It is also essential that once an organizer is completed to help brainstorm the contents of the paper to be written, the student also needs to learn how to take the information from the graphic organizer and create a sequenced outline for the paper. Without the process of moving from the graphic organizer to a sequenced outline, the student's written content may be extremely limited even after he has reviewed many important concepts with the visual tools.

Unfortunately, the majority of our students are extremely reluctant writers and the use of graphic organizers and sequenced outlines require even more written work. However, these visual tools allow a student to learn about *the process* of written expression, rather than simply focus on the written *product* the teacher is expecting to grade. Without the visual tools, in the effort to produce the written product the parent, teacher and/or instructional assistance will likely verbally cue the child through the entire process as a mechanism to try and guide the student through this murky conceptual process. At times parents are brought to the point where they virtually write the paper for the child instead of deal with the frustrations and roadblocks the child experiences during written expression tasks. One parent called me to explain "she got an A- on a paper she had written and she really thought it was A work!" To help a student accept and learn about the value of visual tools across the school day, teachers need to modify their grading of these students to grade their production of the graphic organizers and sequencing outlines as having at least equal value with the written product the visual tools represent. By doing this, the teacher is acknowledging and teaching the student that the process to explore conceptual thinking is at least as important as the written product itself.

It takes persistence to help students learn to use these tools and then see them as a benefit to them since they require additional steps in the learning process. However, these tools are one of the precious few strategies we have available to help students learn about processing the gestalt.

What does studying and scheduling have to do with gestalt processing?

Studying and scheduling require a hefty dose of both organization and prioritizing, especially in the more advanced years of school and certainly college. However, studying is a global concept we assume all children know how to manage. Helping students realize the connection between studying and organizing/prioritizing is important and will also help with initiation of these activities. Some students will say, "I am always studying" while their parents will say, "They never get their homework done." This is a flag to task-analyze what studying means and how to get through it.

Ideas on getting through homework assignments:

1. Studying begins by organizing and then prioritizing general assignments. Simply teaching about these concepts is the first step! Then applying these concepts by introducing an academic planner/calendar book is crucial. **Use of an academic planner to map out assignments for the day *and* over time is essential.** It is really best to track all assignments in one calendar book. Since our students are not organized they have a tendency to want to write things down in all different places!

Sue was a freshman in high school. I asked her about her science class assignment at which point she opened the science book and held it up to the fluorescent light. I could not imagine why she was doing this. It turned out she had written the assignment on the scotch tape that held her book jacket together and the only way to read the blue ink was to illuminate it in the ceiling light!

Helping students to learn reasons why and when to prioritize is important. These ideas can relate to how soon the assignment is due and how important the assignment is to the student's grade.

Ryan's Venn diagram for understanding studying:

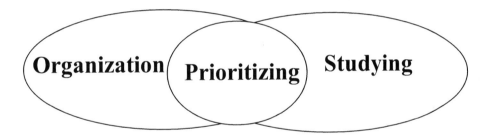

2. Like writing a paper or answering chapter-based questions, studying also has to do with organizing and prioritizing *within the assignment.*

3. Getting through the homework has to do with staying on task! Using visual cueing systems to alert the child to keep working can be helpful. For example, if they have 10 spelling words to write, have them move a poker chip for each word/sentence they need to get through as a self-motivator. Getting through all ten can then earn a ten-minute break.

4. If your student doesn't already, teach him how to "ask for help" at home.

5. If the physical act of writing is a problem, be willing to have him dictate some of his text to you as long as you are willing to write it out as he says it and not greatly revise it! In the case of having him dictate, I prefer that families have the student at least start and end the task, with the adult helping intermittently in the middle depending on the length.

6. If the student is asked to write an assignment on a "blank page" be prepared to help by writing out questions to provide a framework for the assignment and/or through the development of a graphic organizer.

7. For students who work for hours each night, perhaps the homework needs to be modified. This can be done as a modification on the IEP or through a 504 plan if an IEP is not in place. For math and spelling this can happen by having them complete every other problem or word. For a writing assignment this could be reducing the length, but still expecting the child to work towards a level of substance!

8. Remember that our students with social-cognitive deficits are also persons who are going through many if not all of the normal developmental phases of youth. If they develop an "attitude" about homework *and they are motivated to get good grades*, then in some cases allowing them to fail can be a valuable lesson in it itself.

The importance of home-directed schedules:

Studying at home is difficult to accomplish unless the student has a schedule in their brain that allows for such activity. Scheduling is another gestalt-based activity. It is common knowledge that folks with social-cognitive deficits prefer to have schedules; however, if left to their own devices they can create some very unhealthy schedules around their particular areas of interest.

It is also fairly common for these students to develop a mindset that "school is school and home is home, never the two shall meet!" For these children the idea of carrying over assignments into their "place of freedom" is revolting! From an early age explanations and demonstrations of how these environments merge need to be offered by family members. Scheduling for activities can then be accomplished.

Tina was a freshman in high school. Her mother indicated that she did almost nothing to help in the house and teachers were complaining that she did not complete homework assignments. Her response was that she did not have the time. I asked her to write out her home related schedule; she filled an entire binder sheet! Below is a sample from that:

A sample of Tina's self-directed schedule:

At the time Tina was interested in a Vietnamese radio station, I think because she enjoyed listening to the tonal quality of the speech. The "radio" times indicated below were for that station.

2:55-4:35 Free-time
4:30-4:48 TV
5:00-5:30 Dinner
5:31-6:59 Free-time/play tapes
7:00-7:45 Radio
7:46-7:59 Free-time
8:00-8:15 Radio
8:16-8:29 Free-time etc…

From the above schedule it is important to note that Tina's use of the term "free-time" strictly meant that was her time to be without obligation to others. Where we neurotypical adults might look at her schedule and point out that she could fit her responsibilities into her "free-time" slots, this did not make any sense to her.

The lesson learned from the above example is that assistance needs to be provided when scheduling so that the student has to balance his personal interests and priorities with his home and school responsibilities. As I mention in the "perspective taking" section, some expectation of completing chores around the house is as important as completing homework assignments!

Good times to revise schedules include:

1. A couple of days before schools break for a vacation (this is a time to focus on responsibility to the home and other persons living in it).

2. A couple of days before returning to school after the summer vacation. Schedules in school need to balance homework, home chores and need for personal hobby time. It is important to segment out a specific chunk of time for homework and housework, whereby the student cannot return to his personal hobby until that time period has elapsed. If you fail to do this you will get students rushing through their already difficult assignments to get back to playing on the computer, etc.

Points to remember with schedules:

1. All schedules must be written out and posted in a common place! Having a copy in their school binder is also a good idea.
2. Flexibility can also be built into the schedule. "You will do this OR that…"

3. Once you've gone through the time to create a schedule, consistently enforce it! It is much easier to start these types of routines when children are young. While it seems like a lot of work, it will save you endless nagging in the future!

Ideas for Goals and Objective when working on Gestalt Processing:

Goal 1: The student will sequence information with 90% accuracy.

Objective 1: The child will sequence 4 aspects of a story (pictured or written) with 80% accuracy.

Objective 2: The child will create sequences of his own activities with 90% accuracy.

Objective 3: The child will identify missing segments from sequences of one of his own activities with 90% accuracy.

Goal 2: The student will write assignments in his academic planner with 85% accuracy.

Objective 1: The student will write down all daily homework assignments in his academic planner with 85% accuracy, as long as the assignments are posted in class in the same place on a daily basis.

Objective 2: The student will fill out a Project Planning Guide (page 141-143), to organize long-term projects with 85% accuracy with initial cues.

Objective 3: The student will segment long-term projects into daily assignments, and write these components in his planner with 85% accuracy.

Goal 3: The student will make a personal daily schedule and prioritize home and school assignments with 85% accuracy.

Objective 1: The student will take daily chores and assignments and create a list of tasks to complete with 85% accuracy.

Objective 2: The student will take the list of tasks and prioritize them creating a schedule for himself with 85% accuracy.

Objective 3: The student will complete tasks in the order of the priority list 80% of the time.

Goal 4: The student will complete graphic organizers related to core curriculum with 80% accuracy.

Objective 1: The student will fill in the information requested from a prepared graphic organizer with 80% accuracy.

Objective 2: The student will draw the organizational structure of the graphic organizer as he fills in the information with 70% accuracy and minimal cues.

Objective 3: For written expression tasks, the student will use the information presented in the organizer and then complete a sequenced outline with 85% accuracy.

Summary of Chapter 7, Gestalt Processing:

Summary of some ways caregivers can modify the environment to assist with teaching about the gestalt:

1. Provide visual imagery to picture the "whole" and its associated parts.
2. Provide activities where students need to break projects down and then put them back together again, allowing these students extra time for the planning phase!
3. Assist with creating "healthy" schedules for use at home (school already provides a set schedule).
4. Take the time to create Facilitating Frameworks. If an instructional assistant is working with the child, teach them the concept of how to do this.
5. Use graphic organizers creatively.
6. Teach concepts of "brain organization" and prioritizing.
7. Teach the path of "problem solving" using the problem solving worksheet on page 16.
8. Recognize how difficulties with gestalt processing can add to a great amount of confusion in a person's life!

Summary of some activities the student can do to help learn about gestalt processing:

1. Have students look at pictures or review written stories or articles and discuss the relevant vs. the more irrelevant aspects of the item. After that type of discussion:

    a. Have the younger student look at photographs or activity scenes and have him "name the picture" in the same way we give titles to newspaper articles.

b. Have the older student read articles or stories where the title has been removed; have him guess the title. Compare with the original title.

2. Provide sequences of information, and then have them name the sequence. Next remove a piece of the sequence and have them figure out what chunk is missing.

3. Remove a piece of the sequence prior to showing it to them, to see if they can make the connections on their own.

4. Practice using the problem-solving sheet on page 16 to work at identifying the problem and seeing how that lends to a specific set of choices/consequences.

5. Have the student use an academic planner.

6. Teach the child how to create the organization of a graphic organizer.

The following worksheets were developed to help students realize the need to carry over concepts of organization and responsibility from the educational setting to the home.

Name _____ Date _____

PLANNING AND ORGANIZING EVEN WHEN YOU ARE NOT IN SCHOOL!

When you have "free time" at home it is still important that you "fill it" mostly with some type of activity that:

1. You enjoy
    And...
2. Would really help out the people you are living with (this shows you are thinking about others).

But...filling your time this way means you have to organize things in your head.

At the top of the next page, fill out below some things you can do tomorrow during your free time.

 At least one activity should be something you enjoy....and one should be something you do around the house to help someone in your family.

Page 2: Planning and Organizing When at Home

1. _____

2. _____

3. _____

Now that you have chosen some activities, you have to think through...

1. Which one should I do first? (Often we pick the one we least want to do first just to get it over with!)

2. How long should each activity take? This helps you to form a schedule in your head so time does not just slip away.

3. What special tools or equipment do I need to do this? What are they?

4. Do I need to buy something at the store since we don't have it at home? If so, do I need to talk to my parents about money or transportation?

5. Is there a friend I could do this with that would make it more fun? Who should I call? When?

6. If the activity will take more than one day, what is the next time/day I can get back to it?

Plan it!

Write out your schedule for tomorrow:

Include time of day and equipment needs below.

1. _____

_____

2. _____

_____

3. _____

_____

Have fun, let me know how it went!

Name _____ Date_____

Organization...
First the brain has to figure it out...
Then the body has to help out!

List 4 things at HOME that you have to think about organizing...
Then list what you actually have to do with your body to make it get organized...

    1. **Organizing by:**
         a. **Thinking**..._____

         b. **Doing**..._____

    2. **Organizing by:**
         a. **Thinking**..._____

         b. **Doing**..._____

    3. **Organizing by:**
         a. **Thinking**..._____

         b. **Doing**..._____

    4. **Organizing by:**
         a. **Thinking**..._____

         b. **Doing**..._____

List 4 things at SCHOOL or WORK that you have to think about organizing...

1. **Organizing by:**
         a. **Thinking**..._____

         b. **Doing**..._____

    2. **Organizing by:**
         a. **Thinking**..._____

         b. **Doing**..._____

Page 2: Organization

3. **Organizing by:**
    a. **Thinking…** _____

    b. **Doing…** _____

4. **Organizing by:**
    a. **Thinking…** _____

    b. **Doing…** _____

Prioritizing…

Take all 8 things on your home and school list and prioritize them. Which one is the most important? Least important?

1. _____

2. _____

3. _____

4. _____

5. _____

6. _____

7. _____

8. _____

Organizational muck….Where do you get stuck????
What part is the hard part? Thinking or doing?

When you are stuck, what are your choices?

1.

2.

3.

"I LAUGH"

Chapter 8

HUMOR

THIS IS ALL TOO SERIOUS TO BE TAKEN TOO SERIOUSLY!!

When students with social-cognitive deficits appear before us educators for the first time, they often present as being shy, withdrawn and hesitant. At times they give the appearance of being "cold and distant." We are capturing them at their weakest; they have difficulty "reading" new situations and people. At the same time, the results from their standardized tests often show great academic and intellectual accomplishment. It is a confusing situation for an educator. After all, educators are persons who also form impressions of those around them. If a student presents as "cold and smart" then it would be easy to interpret this as "this student does not want to work with me, therefore I will get the lessons done and get him out of my room!" *The catch-22 is that our lessons mean very little if they are not taught in an environment that encourages the development of REAL relationships, including a relationship with the teacher!* ***Humor helps to break the barriers of insecurity and establish a level on which all can relate.***

At the beginning of my journey to determine the factors contributing to my students' success in high school, I had recognized the need for initiation, gestalt thinking, etc., which I presented in the earlier parts of this book. Still, I thought some aspect was missing. Then I heard Dr. Stanley Greenspan give a speech (1998, Keynote address the national Autism Society of America conference, Reno). In that speech he stated "a person needs to be able to relate affectively before he can grow cognitively." I realized at that moment that it was my relationship that I had developed with the students that had allowed them to be open and willing to explore more cognitive concepts; which were challenging for them to learn and discuss. In retrospect, the most important component of our therapy sessions was the unwritten rule that we were allowed to find reason to laugh and relate. At times this meant we would explore humor, but mostly it meant that humor could be introduced, as needed, to liven up a lesson or to take the edge off an embarrassing moment. We could laugh at ourselves and with others. It was OK to laugh at our own mistakes. It was OK to laugh with others when they made mistakes as well.

For some of my students with social-cognitive deficits, the concept of using humor in school was novel and not initially welcomed. After all, we often inadvertently teach our already rigid students how to be more "autistic." From early on in school we insist that "good" students are: quiet, obedient, and suppressive of impulses of humor in the learning environment. While we want all students to follow these general rules of conduct, we also want the students to be relaxed to maximize their focus and minimize their anxiety.

HUMOR RELAXES AND RELEASES!

Timmy had never formally been diagnosed with High Functioning Autism, but he met the diagnostic criteria; he had also never participated in a "social group." He was 14 when I first met him. Timmy was at first concerned by my daily doses of humor, frequently telling me to be serious because I was a teacher. I had worked with him for nearly two years and was discouraged by his lack of progress. He was defensive to touch, thus difficult to approach on all levels. He was always very serious and I felt we never had established much of a relationship. The week before April Fool's Day, we began to study humor as a group. The students were then required to use humor in the group as part of their lesson. The morning of the April Fool's day group, Timmy walked up to where I sat and delivered a huge fake sneeze. I jumped up from the table, ran over to him and made a big deal of how funny he was. He allowed me to touch him! Unbeknownst to me, the formal introduction of humor into the academic environment appeared to validate for Timmy that it was acceptable to use it across this school setting. Literally, from that day forward Timmy laughed and joked with all of us in the group on a regular basis. Remarkably, his attention to auditory tasks also increased as he seemed to feel more as a part of the group, even establishing himself as a group leader monitoring the table conversation of others and instructing them when they interrupted (not all the students appreciated this!). While his progress was of interest to me, the true validation came two weeks later when one of his mainstream teachers approached me and inquired, "What did you do to Timmy?" When I asked what she meant, she explained that he was now independently seeking help and asking questions to clarify information in her class, rather than sitting quietly like he had done previously. Also now noticeably absent was Timmy's extreme tactile defensiveness whenever I approached him. Timmy's development of humor in school truly appeared to relax and release him. He continued onward, forming limited friendships in academic classes, and started sharing his interests with others.

I also learned that the use of humor aids the educator as well. Teaching social relationship skills to persons who are not neurologically wired to excel in this area can be a demanding job!

The first set of high school boys I worked with was a complex group. Two of the five students were selectively mute. Two stuttered, one had Tourette's syndrome; all were on the autism spectrum. When working with older students, each one comes to you with a history of their own issues related to having social-cognitive deficits. Some have been teased horribly; others have lived in pools of confusion. Before teaching can occur, we need to help the group move forward in a positive, supportive way!

While I use humor with all persons I work with, the necessity for humor was actually introduced by this group of students. I had purchased a key chain with a small rubber chicken hanging on it. I always had my keys next to my glass of water where I was to sit at the therapy table. At the beginning of the therapy session I would be scurrying, gathering materials for the session. It was at this time that the boys took advantage of my chicken. They began to hide it, "drown it" in my glass of water, or draw spots on it where spots didn't belong. They did this as a group, laughing together at their mischief. I figured if they enjoyed the chicken we would use it as a therapy tool; the students loved this! A life-sized soft plastic rubber chicken joined my small rubber key chain chicken; each had its place in our sessions. As you can imagine, a rubber chicken is not the essential tool; any small object that has a humorous connotation will do. I have also used trolls, little plastic people figurines, Beanie Babies and overgrown plastic insects.

The following are social-cognitive lessons taught with the aid of rubber chickens:

1. ***"Shouldering the chicken"*** to assist with eye-contact. It is important to teach that while we want students to look towards the face of their communicative partner, we do not

want them to stare into the person's eyes. *Parents have shared with me that two different students had been staring at girls they liked for some time. Subsequently, the police were called in to deal with the apparent "stalking."* People with social-cognitive deficits often have great difficulty looking at other people's eyes.

As a first step in lessons on how to "do" eye-contact, I teach students to look in the direction of a person's face. The key-chain chicken helps to define these limits by sitting on the shoulder of the person who is talking. This serves both as a cue to the speaker as well as the listener that they can look towards a person's head (the area between and above the two shoulders!) and not necessarily into their eyes to maintain healthy eye gaze behavior. This is a far better solution than looking at the bookshelf on the other wall when talking to a partner!

2. ***"Passing the chicken":*** The movement of communication as it passes between communicative partners in verbal exchanges is very abstract! Whose turn is it? How does a conversation move? What exactly is turn-taking? How long should I talk? While we cannot solve all these confusions, we can certainly take this abstract process and help demonstrate its more concrete elements; this is the strength of the chicken!

"Passing the chicken" is introduced as a way to observe how conversations move. It also allows for a person to self-monitor how long they have spoken and give direct feedback that they need to do a specific communicative activity to pass the conversation along to another person. I introduce this concept by making a game out of it. Here are the rules:

a. You pass the chicken by asking a question to another person about that person. (More advanced participants can learn that making related comments or compliments also aid in passing the chicken).

b. The person who receives the chicken answers the question with an elaborated response (beyond a "yes" or "no" answer, since the whole point here is to keep the partners interested in talking to each other!) and then passes the chicken back by asking a related question to the other partner.

c. The chicken "dies" with the following "conversation killers":

    i. The partner who receives the chicken talks on and on, forgetting to maintain the interest of the listener. We generally say the speaker should speak for no more than a minute (for starters). I explain that no matter how interesting our information is to us, a listener's ears can only listen for so long before their "ears get tired." All my students understand this, as I have made their ears tired on many occasions!

    ii. The partner fails to formulate a question back to the listener (even with visual Wh-question cue cards).

    iii. The partner gives an unelaborated answer, giving the speaker nothing more to "run with." For example, when the speaker asks "Do you have any animals?" and the partner answers simply "yes," they have failed to provide the next level to the conversation, which is adding an interesting comment.

When the chicken dies, he flies onto the floor with a thump. It makes for a good laugh and a great lesson. While the chicken may initially die quickly during the first couple of attempts, it is amazing to see how quickly students can learn to build more appropriate responses and remember to pass the conversation back and forth. A mother shared with me that she was able to use this concept (chicken-less) in the community, when her child was expected to produce a conversational response to a less familiar person, yet failed to respond. She whispered to him "pass the chicken"; that was enough information to cue him to formulate a response and ask a return question.

3. *"Nipping with the chicken"* requiring the use of the larger rubber chicken. This very sophisticated technique is used when students are self-monitoring and controlling some very specific skills we have reviewed. For example, if a student is working on maintaining eye-gaze towards the speaker, yet he looks away, the chicken may "nip" him in the shoulder. This is yet one more "nag-less" prompt to attend to specific skills. While this sounds a bit intrusive, most students really enjoy the chicken intervening, rather than the adult. I also allow the students to use the chicken to "nip" me back when my social behavior is less than stellar.

Who says these students lack empathy?

I used to jokingly call this nipping process "hitting kids with the chicken" and I explained it at a workshop I gave for parents. A mother then told her 9-year-old son, who was coming to work with me, "you are going to love working with Mrs. Winner, and she hits kids with a chicken!" As I walked in to meet the student he picked up my life-sized rubber chicken and powerfully whipped me with it. When I got over my shock I responded, "What did you do that for?" He replied, "That is for all the kids you have hit with the chicken!!" I have now changed my wording!

To avoid losing sight of the fact that these students tend to also be quite concrete in their learning, lessons are also required related to when humor is NOT APPROPRIATE or welcomed. Exploring what makes some people laugh, and what definitely doesn't is a worthy discussion.

I worked with Tyler, who was 19 and about to graduate from high school. He had no friends and his mother reported that this discouraged and depressed him. Tyler attempted to use a lot of sarcastic and disgusting humor. He reported that this made others laugh. He interpreted this to mean that he was "cool" and that people liked him when he was funny. As part of the group he was in, we watched a portion of the cartoon show called Southpark. We discussed why it was funny; namely because the humor was so unexpected (3ʳᵈ grade children talking in rude ways about crude themes). We also discussed that some of the time people laugh not because they think someone is particularly funny, but because they make us feel uncomfortable. After the discussion about Southpark, Tyler again volunteered that he made people laugh. When I gently pointed out that he also had no friends, he responded, "I think I am starting to get it."

Summary, Chapter 8, Humor

Humor is simply a tool to establish and maintain a real relationship. Having an ear open to listen and words to support are also critical elements.

This is not only important to teach, *but important to incorporate into how we teach!*

Chapter 9

Thoughts On Reading Comprehension

Comprehension of literature is not significantly different from the knowledge required for comprehension of our daily social interactions; it requires social knowledge as well!

Reading comprehension requires us to:

1. Decode the text into a language we can interpret. Most, but not all of our students are excellent decoders. With the more typical special education population in our schools, reading problems noted are generally because the student has difficulty decoding. Our students, with social-cognition deficits, tend to have more difficulty with comprehending the reading. There are relatively few treatment programs available to help with reading comprehension difficulties. Lindamood-Bell is one therapeutic technique that is effective helping to remediate comprehension problems (www.lindamoodbell.com).

2. Understand the motives and personality of the characters. This requires heavy doses of perspective taking.

3. Predict problems that may arise and generate possible solutions. Typical readers ask questions to themselves about how they think the novel will advance,

intermittently throughout their reading. Our students don't often do that!

4. Following the overall theme or gestalt of the book.

Reading achievement tests in schools are considered to accurately assess a student's reading comprehension skills, however from my anecdotal experiences I feel that they greatly fall short of that goal. Most standardized reading tests require the reading of relatively short passages and/or assess comprehension through multiple-choice questions. The structure offered by these questions as well as the brevity of the passage provides enough information for our students to pass with flying colors. These same students often cannot begin to analyze and interpret the meaning of an age-appropriate novel.

If it is recognized that a student has difficulties with reading comprehension, we tend to write the generic goal "the student will comprehend the main idea and list 3 supporting details" as a means for helping the student learn to comprehend. Just as with concepts "communicative effectiveness" and "problem solving," "determining the main idea" is very vague. Instead we need to be writing goals that relate back to the same type of social thinking we are teaching the students to explore in other aspects of their life; namely a focus on perspective taking, problem solving, inferencing and understanding the gestalt! If we can approach reading comprehension in much the same way we approach the comprehension of real social relationships, I believe, we will help our students understand these global concepts more fully.

Goals and Objectives:

The following are ideas of goals and objectives that help to guide the student through the process of reading comprehension from a social-cognitive point of view.

Goal 1: The student will be able to explain a character's personality and perspective and how they change or remain the same over the course of the book, using examples from the text with 80% accuracy.

Objective 1: Chapter by chapter, the student will describe the main character's personality, mood and thoughts, giving examples of each from the written text, with 80% accuracy.

Objective 2: Chapter by chapter, the student will describe how the main character relates to other characters in the book according to the words spoken and his actions, using examples from the text with 80% accuracy.

Objective 3: Chapter by chapter, the student will describe if the different settings or contexts affect the personality of the character, using examples from the text with 80% accuracy.

Goal 2: The student will be able to explain the main problem or set of problems the characters in the book encountered, and how the chosen solution affected the overall story, with 80% accuracy.

Objective 1: The student will define each problem with 80% accuracy.

Objective 2: The student will identify the choice the character made to solve the problem as well as one other possible choice the character could have considered, with 90% accuracy.

Objective 3: The student will discuss possible story outcomes if a different choice had been made for the identified problem(s) with 80% accuracy.

Summary:
Chapter 9
Thoughts on Reading
Comprehension

Reading comprehension is often difficult for our students, as it requires skills in all of the areas covered in the I LAUGH approach. Most techniques used in schools to enhance reading comprehension focus on the student identifying the main idea and supporting details, but this approach fails to reach our students' needs. Our students need to be encouraged to explore literature in the same way that we are encouraging them to explore social thinking; by investigating the processes of problem solving and communicative effectiveness. This includes a thorough investigation of the perspective of the primary characters in the book.

Included in this chapter are some examples of goals and objectives that can be used in IEPs to facilitate this type of social thinking.

Chapter 10

THOUGHTS ON OBSERVING A STUDENT'S SOCIAL SKILLS AND SOCIAL RELATEDNESS

I was at an elementary school to consult with an educational team regarding Ron, a 9-year-old boy with Asperger Syndrome. He had come a long way in a year, learning to interact with peers. The staff was proud of his accomplishments, especially of the fact that he no longer walked the perimeter of the playground, but now fully engaged in activities with peers during recess. I went out to observe Ron playing with his friends during the morning break. He was, indeed, on the large grass field amidst a group of boys gathered around a football. I was impressed that Ron was right in there actively engaged in a discussion to organize a football game. As the game began, I noticed how Ron followed the ball with his eyes but did not run in the direction of the ball. Instead, once another boy caught the ball, he walked towards the ball pointing to his chest and yelling what appeared to me to be "I want the football!" "It's my turn," "Give me the football" in hopes the boys would let him initiate the next throw. He continued this same process of staying on the field with the boys and verbally commanding the ball in his direction, with the catch of each ball. He never athletically pursued the ball on his own. On occasion (about 1 of every 4 turns), one of the boys would give Ron the ball to throw for the next play. This however, did not cause him to yield his verbal commands; he continued to yell for the ball to be given to him throughout the entire recess. Ron was playing his own game of "verbal football."

The above example demonstrates how a casual observer could perceive that our student, Ron, was appropriately engaged with his peers during recess. However, more skilled observation demonstrated that Ron's attempts to engage with peers was actually inappropriate to the situation and clearly not a behavior other students would tolerate for many months.

As professionals, we can spend many hours and great effort pouring over our test results trying to determine an appropriate diagnosis for a student; meanwhile, his peers have already reached their own conclusions!

We can only provide therapeutic services to students in the schools if they qualify for services. This is often tricky given that many of our students perform exceptionally well on the structured standardized tests, even though they are often far less able to demonstrate appropriate skills in functional settings.

One option that is available as part of a total assessment is for a skilled observer (psychologist, speech language pathologist, social worker, etc.) to complete a social-pragmatic-language sample of a student. This provides information to the assessment team beyond the solitude and structure of the test environment. It allows us to explore a student's application of his skills in real communicative situations.

An observation has its ground rules:

1. **The student must be observed with same-aged peers.** Our students often prefer the tolerance of older kids or their

ability to lead younger children, but are often not sure how to relate to same-aged peers.

2. **The student and the other children should not know you are there to watch him.**
3. **The student should be observed across 3 different settings** (e.g. classroom, lunch and recess).

When observing note the following aspects:

Observations of the students' activity:

1. Does the student maintain a close proximity to other peers?
2. Does the student maintain body language that indicates he is a member of the activity?
3. Does the student cooperate in the activity in much the same way as the other peers, or does he appear to be "marching to a different drummer?"
4. Does the student engage in a variety of activities, or prefer to stay with the same activity regardless of what the peers do?
5. Does the student recognize the structure and order of the activity he is participating in?
6. Does the student look like he is enjoying himself?
7. Did the student select this activity, or was he told he was to do it?

Observations of the Student's language Use:

1. Does the student initiate language with peers? This is very different from watching him respond to peers.
2. Does the student ask questions to other children about the other children (e.g. What did you do last night?).
3. Does the student negotiate with others? If not does he remain silent or is he bossy, demanding they do it his way?
4. Does the student engage in reciprocal communication with peers?
5. Does the student attend to what the other children are saying when it is their turn to talk?

6. Does the student use non-verbal components of language when engaging with others? (e.g. eye-contact, body language, gestures, tone of voice, etc..)

Observations of the other children's reaction to the student:

1. Do other children appear to notice that the student is different in his interactions or participation?
2. Do the other children comment about the student or tease him?
3. Do the other children appear to make accommodations for the student?
4. Do the other children continue to play with the student, or do they go off to engage in a different activity?

Completing a narrative assessment...

Completing an assessment of social-pragmatic skills would also involve interviewing the classroom teacher regarding her observations of the student.

The parents are also a really valid source of information regarding their child's social development. Parents are often frustrated that school personnel do not seek their observations of their own child more actively. I consider these students "24 hour a day kids," meaning that their disability continues across the hours of the day regardless of the setting, requiring a team approach, which strongly includes the parents.

Chapter 11

TEACHING SO OUR TEACHING STICKS!

Summary of ten considerations for applying concepts related to social-cognition into our therapeutic group work.

It is one thing to know WHAT to teach and a completely different concept to know HOW to teach it! While most formal education consists of the teacher directing lessons from the front of the class for the students to consider alone at their desks, this format does not assist the growth of truly functional skills for persons with social-cognitive deficits. Concepts and skills related to social-cognition cannot be taught from the podium, they need to be taught in "real time" while experiencing a real relationship with another person. This is truly the benefit of having "social skills groups."

Below are 10 suggestions on how to strengthen concepts related to social-cognition in therapy groups that assist in maximizing carryover to other situations.

1. **Tell WHAT you are teaching the child BEFORE you try to teach it, and WHY a strategy is being taught.**

   The social-cognitive information we want the students to learn is incredibly abstract. Yet, the same information that we are teaching them (skills for conversations, etc.) has been modeled for them thousands of times. If the students were going to acquire it naturally they would have done it by now! Since we need to teach social thinking and related skills, we need to do so in a very up-front manner to help the student learn how he is to focus his attention. These students are concrete thinkers; they do not actively search for hidden meanings nor pull social information together well on their own.

   We also need to move away from believing that our social groups are simply teaching "social skills" and move towards focusing on enhancing "social-cognition." A social skill is a superficial component of a social interaction; a device to help these students engage in behavior that appears more socially acceptable. We all want our students to learn all these skills, however teaching only at the skill level is not enough. If we don't teach them *WHY* they are learning a skill it is difficult for them to generalize this into a social concept that can be applied across a number of different situations.

   For example, I observed a 9-year-old boy during his speech therapy session. His therapist taught him about the social skill of "using compliments." She gave him the example "I like your shirt." The boy then practiced this compliment telling each person sitting at the table that he liked their shirt. The therapist then told him his homework was to go home and give his mother a compliment and she asked if he could do that. The boy agreed he could. I then asked the boy why he would give someone a compliment, he replied after a silent pause "I don't know" (he did not understand the underlying social concept!).

A student should always know WHY to use a concept before he is taught HOW to use a skill!

2. **How do we teach our abstract lessons so that the students can grasp them?**

Teaching these students takes extra skill and knowledge. One of the many useful tricks is learning how to break concepts down into finer and finer pieces to a point where the student can first comfortably grasp the information. Defining concepts at their most basic elements allows us to teach abstract information by presenting it in concrete segments that eventually grow more abstract. For example, when teaching a child how a conversation moves we can teach them about the concept of "turn-taking" but this remains too abstract for virtually most of our students (regardless of age!). A basic concrete lesson is to demonstrate turn-taking by using a familiar object (I use a rubber chicken). Instruct the participant that the first person to speak "passes the chicken" (and conversation) to the other person by asking a question to that person. The person who just received the chicken (and conversation) now answers the question and then passes the conversation (and chicken) back to the listener by asking him a question. This procedure can continue an unlimited number of times, as both participants learn to actively formulate answers and questions when holding the chicken, and actively listen when waiting to receive the chicken. This is a very basic, concrete lesson that can be used to enforce social thinking and related skills including:
- Taking perspective
- Formulating questions

- Providing responses that are neither too vague nor too complex
- Turn-taking
- Topic maintenance
- Eye-contact, etc.

The strength of this type of lesson is the concrete object allows us to "stop and focus" on aspects of communication that had been "invisible" before.

Other tools for helping to develop a concrete understanding of abstract lessons include:
- Visually presented lessons.
- Minimize long verbal explanations; the more verbal we are in our explanations the more abstract they are likely to become. *Although this population is highly verbal it is generally not their best mode of learning!*
- Don't hurry through lessons; allow time to break down concepts. Quality teaching and thinking takes time!

3. Teach the fundamental, gestalt based concepts first and refer back to them with each session.

There are many, many components related to developing good social skills (over 60!). Since our students don't easily infer how pieces of information fit together, it is important that we constantly keep them plugged in to how a concept we are teaching relates to a concept already learned!

The acronym "TOPS" helps to describe to students the range of areas they most likely will have difficulty with. It also provides them with categories that all other skills and concepts fit directly into. There is certainly overlap between the categories, and some skills share more than one category, for example: "personal problem solving" almost always involves some aspect of each of the categories.

However, it is important for the students to be introduced to some global frames of reference from which they can learn some basic principles and related skills.

I use the acronym TOPS as the first element of curriculum in the social therapy groups. It is posted on the walls of the therapy room, and referred back to as needed across future sessions. On page 195-196 are worksheets I give to students to explore the meaning of TOPS.

T = Taking Perspective: Thinking about others and how they think about you.
O = Organizing and Prioritizing, using your brain!
P = Personal Problem Solving
S = Social Thinking and Social Skills

4. Socially interact during the sessions.

In an effort to learn the skills written in the IEP or keep pace with the curriculum being used, we at times lose sight of the original intent of the group as being to facilitate social interaction and learn to develop social relationships. This relationship depends on how the group leader relates to the group. I believe the group leader should be considered as part of the group, including sharing her emotional states and perspective as they relate to the group. On days where I was glum for one reason or another, I would inform the group about my emotional state - "I have had a rough day and am not in a good mood!" I would then ask the students how they are expected to relate to me that day given my mood. During this time usually a student would respond, "We have to behave today!" I would agree, stating that I would have much less patience today because of my mood. By the same token, if I was in a particularly bubbly mood, some student would acknowledge that they could "get away with more" that day. I would agree with that as well.

I would also share my perspective about other group members. If a person in the group were being particularly dynamic one day, I would pose a question to the group about how that person is making me feel. On the other hand, if a student in the group were challenging that day, I would pose the same question. This helped the students to realize that their behavior, directly communicative or not, affects social interactions and relationships. All students are encouraged to both share their emotional experiences or moods as well as reactions to behavioral states of other individuals in the group. This actually helps to create a more cooperative attitude when students know they will be accountable for their behaviors!

5. **Start each session with a "check-in."**

All social groups should begin the session with social experiences. Starting each group with a "conversational check-in" is a great way to socially touch base. Prior to the "check-in" is an ideal time to review social thinking concepts and related skills previously discussed in other lessons. I have the group brainstorm about concepts and skills that need to be considered and employed to have a successful social interaction. We list these ideas on the wipe-away board and pose group challenges to see how many minutes or passes-of-the-chicken the group can maintain without me having a "naggable moment." This type of instruction also fosters self-evaluation of the social thinking and related skills needed to succeed in the "real world." This check-in can last for 10-15 minutes, but it is generally a very rich learning time as social thinking and skills are applied in a realistic context.

6. Teach to the moment
Always have a curriculum plan and always be ready to toss it aside for the day.

Knowing the concepts you want to address in a session is a good idea (as opposed to winging it, which is not such a hot idea). However, our students are most apt to learn the real lessons when they relate to them directly. After I have introduced the acronym TOPS (discussed above) in one of my first lessons, I now have license to introduce any subject at any time that relates to any of those four issues. Thus, I may plan a lesson on "friendship" but when a student comes to the group with a huge problem related to how to approach a teacher to discuss an assignment he doesn't understand, it is now time to DROP EVERYTHING AND ATTEND TO THAT STUDENT'S NEEDS!

Helping students to break down (task analyze) how to evaluate choices, consider perspectives, approach a teacher and formulate language is a huge part of the communicative and problem solving process. At the same time, other members of the group see a "real" problem play out and can share their ideas adding validity to the real issues you are trying to teach as well as allowing for team building.

This type of instruction does require flexibility on the part of the group leader. I like to joke "School is autism…. Across the day we have a bell schedule, seating chart, change topics for no logical reason and we have an inflexible adherence to routine!" All the while we need to teach flexibility to our students!

While curricula are endlessly useful in directing us towards greater avenues of teaching, they take on a temporal life of their own. We feel compelled to move at a pace to cover curriculum rather than meet the child's need of really understanding and integrating the information presented.

Allow yourself the freedom to slow down and teach towards quality understanding and interactions.

7. Isolate specific behaviors for students to track.

The bottom line is that students participate in social therapy groups because modifications need to be made to their social regulation and discourse related behaviors. By participating in a social-cognitive group it is hoped that the students will increase their insight into the process, but will also be able to modify how they react in social environments. Each student has some behavior that can be tracked that will help with his participation in the social world. For some children this may mean tracking a behavior that is an obvious annoyance to fellow members of the group (kicking fellow students under the table) but for other students it may be a very high-level participation skill such as "providing a related comment" when another person is speaking. Each person in the group is expected to track a different behavior to emphasize the differences in people (we don't all share the exact same issues!) and to provide the participants discrete aspects to focus on while reviewing a more general lesson as part of the whole group.

I track individuals' behaviors on large index cards. I will write out the behavior a specific student needs to modify on the card and stick it in front of him. Along with this is also a short discussion defining the behavior and why it is appropriate to place it on the card. I also write a card out for me that states, "Do not interrupt" (that is my bad habit!). I then teach the kids the process of changing a behavior explaining that behavior change has 3 components:

1. Self-awareness: When you are aware that you have this behavior to focus on modifying.

2. Self-monitoring: When you watch yourself do the behavior. I describe, "monitoring" as being like a computer monitor, in that you watch it. In this case you are watching yourself!

3. Self-control: This is when you are actually in charge of controlling your own behavior. Often this is the reward phase of the behavior plan.

During the awareness and monitoring phases of using the index cards to track behaviors I will put a star or smiley face on the cards of the younger kids when they are doing a good job improving their behavior. With middle school students and above I generally reverse the process and put a small tear in the edge of the card when they "blow it." When I place a "happy face" or tear on their cards I do not need to verbally elaborate, keeping the behavioral plan minimally intrusive to the more general lesson of the day.
I am the person tracking their behavior since they are still at the awareness and monitoring phases of their behavior management. They are free to track my behavior in the same way and they do! When the students are proficient at recognizing their behaviors they can then begin the self-control phase where they get to monitor their own cards by giving themselves rewards or rips.

The worksheet on the following page can be used as a self-monitoring sheet.

Name_____ Date_____

CHECKING MY OWN BEHAVIORS!

1. SELF-AWARENESS: I need to increase my awareness of: (write down a behavior you are trying to get rid of!)

_____

If I am on the self-awareness phase, then my teacher will "nag" me to pay attention to this behavior.

2. SELF-MONITOR: I can monitor my behavior by thinking about it. When I think about it I can begin to control it!

_____

If I am on the self-monitoring phase, then I should be paying attention to my behavior all by myself, my teacher might remind me to pay attention to it!

3. SELF-CONTROL: I can control my behavior by:

_____

If I am in the self-control phase, then I should be able to control this behavior myself most of the time. My teacher might remind me that I should be in charge of controlling it!

8. **Teach perspective taking**:

Taking perspective of others and ourselves is an extremely challenging component for our students. However, from my clinical work, I see that students with Asperger Syndrome or Non-Verbal Learning Disabilities have the best prognosis for grasping aspects of this concept. But, how do we teach it? As stated above we need to take an abstract concept and break it down to its most concrete components. For perspective taking I believe the first step is realizing we all make impressions. We make impressions based on three things:

   i. **How you look:** This relates to dress and hygiene
   ii. **What you say:** This refers to only the words we use, which carry about 20-40% of the meaning.
   iii. **What you do:** This refers to all those other dynamics of communication such as body language, facial expression, tone, inflection and loudness of voice, gestures, proximity, eye-contact, etc.

After this initial lesson the students will keep journals on impressions they think they make upon others and impressions people make upon them based on these 3 components. I also help students to stay accountable to their behavior in the group by discussing those who are making "good" impressions or "poor" impressions based on one of these specific attributes. In future lessons I go on to discuss higher levels of perspective taking (e.g. perspective has memory, perspective taking requires us to pick up on contextual cues, etc.). However, this first lesson on making impressions launches many discussions related to how the different social-cognitive lessons and skills being taught in the group affect people's perspectives of you and your perspective of them.

9. Use humor!

Persons with social-cognitive deficits seem particularly gifted with a great sense of humor. For some students who lack facial expression or deal with high-levels of anxiety the teacher may have to initially search for the humor inside the person, but it is a hunt well worth the time! *This disability is too serious to take too seriously.* Humor appears to be an effective way of "relaxing and releasing."

Humor allows us to engage at a more personal level. Those of us leading social groups are teaching about the positive aspects of socially connecting, therefore we have to allow for the social connections to happen in a natural and enjoyable way. Pages in curriculum do not offer this element. As group leaders we need to show that we can be related to, picked apart and understood just as we plan to do to the students!

Goofy props such as a rubber chicken lighten up the mood and take the edge off the seriousness of the lesson. Humor can also easily be employed using Carol Gray's Comic Strip Conversations. At times it is simply just allowing for the joke to be told or the misinterpretation of the moment to be laughed at. If we can't laugh at ourselves then there is no humor! As I talk about humor being part of our lessons I don't mean going in search of presenting all lessons through funny jokes, it is more about bringing warmth, compassion and humor as an attitude that pervades every session.

10. Feel good about running non-integrated social-cognition groups!

In the push to keep children in the mainstream there is pressure to mainstream every aspect of interaction. If our children were going to learn social-cognition and related skills by modeling the behaviors of others they would not have these problems! By running non-integrated groups (e.g. groups made up only of kids with deficits in social-cognition) our students are able to talk about their experiences and be related to by others with the same experience. Our students do have empathy and feelings; they don't like always not knowing and not understanding how persons who are socially gifted think. Our groups have a "support group" quality. By bringing in neuro-typical peers our students would not be allowed the freedom to share their feelings as well as take the time to task analyze concepts down to the infinitesimal parts that most typical folks can't imagine we even have to discuss.

At the same time not all of our students can be grouped together; this is still a very broad spectrum with an array of functioning levels and personalities. Successful groups need to be created carefully and nurtured all along the way. Once the students get to a place that they can begin to produce more appropriate skills then it is ideal to have them seek activities in the "mainstream," in addition to the group, where they can carryover skills and self-monitor their progress.

A final note: as we begin to work with students on learning abstract concepts such as perspective taking and relational skills we need to allow them time to process the information. Avoid expecting to see progress in their relationships right away. *Time is needed to process and integrate the information.*

About the worksheets:

On the following pages are worksheets to help students learn about the TOPS acronym. As mentioned above, I recommend starting therapy groups with this concept.

The worksheet on the next page is simply to review the acronym and what each component means. At the bottom of this worksheet, the students are guided to think more about perspective taking, as that is the one most difficult concepts to define.

On those lines students should write responses such as:

-by asking them questions about others
-by listening to the answers of others
-by looking at other's facial expressions
-by understanding the meaning of other's tone of voice
-by watching their body language
-by remembering what others told you before
-etc…

Name_____ Date_____

TOPS

T: **Thinking about how others think….Perspective!**

O: **Organization**

P: **Problem Solving**

S: **Social Participation**

T: Thinking about others = Facts and Feelings
How do you learn about how others think?

      1._____

         _____

      2._____

         _____

      3._____

Name_____

TOPS Worksheet:

_A._ List what the initial means.

_B._ Give one example.

T: A. _____

   B. _____

O: A. _____

   B. _____

P: A. _____

   B. _____

S: A. _____

   B. _____

BIBLIOGRAPHY &
Recommended Therapy Materials

American Psychiatric Association (1994). *Diagnostic and Statistical Manual of Mental Disorders (DSM-1V)*, 4th ed. Washington DC. APA.

Attwood, T. (1998). Asperger's Syndrome, A guide for Parents and Professionals. Jessica Kingsley Publishers: London and Philadelphia.

Baron-Cohen, S. (1995). Mindblindness: An Essay on Autism and Theory of Mind. The MIT Press: Massachusetts

Boucher, J. & Lewis, V. (1989) Memory Impairments and Communication in Relatively Able Autistic Children. *Journal of Child Psychology and Psychiatry, 30, No.1*, 99-122.

Burack, J. and Volkmar, F. (1992) Development of Low- and High-Functioning Autistic Children. *Journal of Child Psychology and Psychiatry, 33, No. 3*, 607-616.

Cumine, V., Leach, J. & Stevenson, G. (1998) Asperger Syndrome, A Practical Guide for Teachers. David Fulton Publishers, London

Ehlers, S., Nyden, A., Gillberg, C.; Sandberg, A., Dahlgren, S., Hjelmquist, E. and Oden, A. (1997) Asperger Syndrome, Autism and Attention Disorders: A Comparative Study of the Cognitive Profiles of 120 Children. *Journal of Child Psychology and Psychiatry, 38, No. 2*, 207-217.

Frith, U. (1989) *Autism: Explaining the Enigma*. Oxford. Basil Blackwell Ltd.

Frith, U. (1991) Autism and Asperger's Syndrome. Great Britain: Cambridge University Press

Fullerton, A., Stratton, J., Coyne, P., & Gray, S. (1996). *Higher Functioning Adolescents and Young Adults with Autism*. Austin, Texas. PRO-ED, Inc.

Freeman, S. and Drake, L: (1997) Teach Me Language and Teach Me Language Companion Manual, SKF Books, Canada.

Gerber, A. (1993) Language-Related Learning Disabilities, Their Nature and Treatment. Paul H. Brookes: Baltimore.

Gillberg, I. and Gillberg, C. (1989) Asperger Syndrome - Some Epidemiological Considerations: A Research Note. *Journal of Child Psychology and Psychiatry, 30, No.4*, 631-638.

Gray, C. (1994). The Original Social Story Book and Social Stories…All New Stories Teaching Social Skills. Future Horizons Publisher: Tx. www.futurehorizons-autism.com

Green, J. (1990) Is Asperger's Syndrome? *Developmental Medicine and Child Neurology, 32,* 743-747.

Greenspan, S. (1998) Keynote Speaker at the Autism Society of America National Convention: July, Reno, Nevada.

Happe, F. (1994) *Autism: An Introduction to Psychological Theory.* Cambridge, MA: Harvard University Press.

Howlin, P., Baron-Cohen, S., Hadwin, J. (1999) Teaching Children with Autism to Mind Read, A practical guide. Wiley and Sons: New York.

Hughes, C., Russell, J., & Robbins, T. (1994) Evidence For Executive Dysfunction in Autism. *Neuropsychologia, 32,* 477-492.

Journal of Autism and Related Developmental Disabilities, (Can be ordered through the Autism Society of America) Plenum Press: New York.

Kazak, S., Collis, G. & Lewis, V. (1997) Can Young People with Autism Refer to Knowledge States? Evidence from Their Understanding of "Know" and "Guess". *Journal of Child Psychology and Psychiatry, 38, No. 8,* 1001-1009.

Krantz, P. & McClannahan, L. (1993) Teaching Children With Autism To Initiate To Peers: Effects Of A Script-Fading Procedure. *Journal of Applied Behavior Analysis, 26,* 121-132.

Levine, M. (1980) The Language Parts Catalogue; Educators Publishing Services: Cambridge. www.epsbooks.com

McEvoy, R.; Rogers, S. and Pennington, B. (1993) Executive Function and Social Communication Deficits in Young Autistic Children. *Journal of Child Psychology and Psychiatry, 34, No. 4,* 563-578.

Minshew, N, Goldstein, G. (1998) Autism As A Disorder Of Complex Information Processing. Mental Retardation and Developmental Disabilities Research Reviews. Vol. *4*: 129-136

Minshew, N., Goldstein, G., Muenz, L., & Payton, J. (1992) Neuropsychological Functioning in Nonmentally Retarded Autistic Individuals. *Journal of Clinical and Experimental Neuropsychology, 14, No.5,* 749-761.

Morgan, H. (1996) *Adults with Autism: A Guide to Theory and Practice.* Cambridge. Cambridge University Press.

Myles, B. & Southwick, J. (1999) Asperger Syndrome and Difficult Moments. www.futurehorizons.com

Ozonoff, S., Pennington, B. & Rogers, S. (1991) Executive Function Deficits in High-Functioning Autistic Individuals: Relationship to Theory of Mind. *Journal of Child Psychology and Psychiatry, 32, No.7*, 1081-1105.

Ozonoff, S., Rogers, S. and Pennington, B. (1991) Asperger's Syndrome: Evidence of an Empirical Distinction from High-Functioning Autism. *Journal Of Child Psychology and Psychiatry, 32, No. 7*, 1107-1122.

Quill, K. (1997) Instructional Considerations for Young Children with Autism: The Rationale for Visually Cued Instruction. Journal of Autism and Developmental Disorders, 27, No. 6, 697-714.

Richard, G. (1997) The Source For Autism. LinguiSystems: Illinois

Rouke, B. (1989) Nonverbal Learning Disabilities: The Syndrome and the Model. Guilford Press: New York.

Rumsey, J. (1985) Conceptual Problem-Solving in Highly Verbal, Nonretarded Autistic Men. Journal of Autism and Developmental Disorders, 15, No. 1, 23-36.

Rumsey, J. & Hamburger, S. (1988) Neuropsychological Findings in High-Functioning Men with Infantile Autism, Residual State. *Journal of Clinical and Experimental Neuropsychology, 10, No. 2*, 201-221.

Rumsey, J. & Hamburger, S. (1990) Neuropsychological Divergence of High-Level Autism and Severe Dyslexia. *Journal of Autism and Developmental Disorders, 20, No. 2*, 155-167.

Russell, J. (1997) *Autism As An Executive Disorder*. Oxford. Oxford University Press.

Schopler, E. (1996) Ask the Editor: Are Autism and Asperger Syndrome Different Labels or Different Disabilities? *Journal of Autism and Developmental Disorders, 26, No. 1*, 109- 110.

Schopler, E. & Mesibov, G. (1992) *High-Functioning Individuals with Autism*. New York. Plenum Press.

Schopler, E.; Mesibov, G. (1998) Asperger Syndrome or High Functioning Autism? Plenum Press: New York.

Shah, A. and Frith, U. (1983) An Islet of Ability in Autistic Children: A Research Note. *Journal of Child Psychology and Psychiatry, 24, No. 4*, 613-620.

Shah, A. and Frith, U. (1993) Why Do Autistic Individuals Show Superior Performance on the Block Design Task? Journal of Child Psychology and Psychiatry, 34, No.8, 1351-1364.

Siegel, D., Minshew, N & Goldstein, G (1996) Wechsler IQ Profiles in Diagnosis of High-Functioning Autism. *Journal of Autism and Developmental Disorders, 26, No. 4,* 389-406.

Szatmari, P., Bartolucci, G. & Bremner, R. (1989) Asperger's Syndrome and Autism: comparison of Early History and Outcome. *Developmental Medicine and Child Neurology, 31,* 709-720.

Thompson, S. (1997) The Source for Nonverbal Learning Disorders LinguiSystems: Illinois

Van Bourgondien, M. & Mesibov, G. (1987) Humor in High-Functioning Autistic Adults. *Journal of Autism and Developmental Disorders, 17, No. 3.,* 417-424.

Wainwright-Sharp, J and Bryson, S. (1993) Visual Orienting Deficits in High-Functioning People with Autism. *Journal of Autism and Developmental Disorders, 23, No. 1,* 1-13.

Wiig, E. and Wilson, C. (1998) Visual Tools for Language and Communication: Content, Use and Interaction. Applied Symbolix, Inc. 1-800-676-7551

Wiley, L. (1999) Pretending To Be Normal: Living with Asperger Syndrome. Jessica Kingsley Publishers: London.

Williams, D. (1992) Nobody No Where: The Extraordinary Autobiography of An Autistic. New York: Avon.

Wing, L. (1981) Asperger's Syndrome: A Clinical Account. *Psychological Medicine, 11,* 115-129.

Wing, L. (1986) Letters to the Editor: Clarification on Asperger's Syndrome. *Journal of Autism and Developmental Disorders, 16, No. 4,* 513-515.

Winner, M. (2002) *Thinking About You Thinking About Me.* www.socialthinking.com

Winner, M. (2005) *Think Social! A Social Thinking Curriculum for Teaching School Age Students.* www.socialthinking.com

Winner, M. (2005) *Worksheets! for Teaching Social Thinking and Related Skills.* www.socialthinking.com

Therapy Materials

Educators Publishing Service, Inc (EPS), Year 2000 catalog with information on products from Dr. Mel Levine, 31 Smith Place, Cambridge, Massachusetts, 02138-1089; 1-800-225-5750

Flynn, K. (1995) Graphic Organizers…helping children to think visually. Creative Teaching Press, Inc., Cypress, CA.

Gajewski, N. & Mayo, P. (1998). Social Skill Strategies: A Curriculum for Adolescents; Books A and B. Thinking Publications, Wisconsin. www.thinkingpublications.com

Gajewski, N. & Mayo, P. (1987). Transfer Activities: Thinking Skill Vocabulary Development. Thinking Publications, Wisconsin. www.thinkingpublications.com

Gray, B. (1990) Problem Solving for Teens; An Interactive Approach to Real Life Problem Solving. LinguiSystems: Illinois. www.linguisystems.com

Gray, C. (1994) Comic Strip Conversations. Future Horizons, Tx. www.futurehorizons-autism.com

Murphy, C. (1985) Adult Reading Series, New Reader's Press; Books 3 and 5. Syracuse, New York. (This series was written for ESL students but has good inferential reading and figurative language in these page long stories).

Parks, S. and Black, H. (1992) Organizing Thinking, Books 1 and 2. Critical Thinking Books and Software: Pacific Grove, CA. www.criticalthinking.com

Pro•Ed (1990s) "Emotions and Expressions: Photographs." Search in Online Catalog of Products. www.proedinc.com

Speechmark Publishing (2005) Color Cards® Sequencing. Sequences: 6 & 8-Step for Children; Sequences: 6 & 8-Step for Adults. www.speechmark.net

Time Timer, Generaction. 513-561-2599 www.timetimer.com

Wiig, E. and Wilson, C. (2001) Map It Out. Thinking Publications, Eau Claire, WI. www.thinkingpublications.com

Winner, M. (2003) "Social Thinking Across the Home and School Day." 4 hour DVD: 2 hours of a workshop summarizing this book and 2 hours of Michelle doing therapy with students. www.socialthinking.com

Winner, M. (2002) *Thinking About You Thinking About Me.* www.socialthinking.com

Winner, M. (2005) "Organizing Strategies for Homework and the Real World." 3.5 hour DVD providing Michelle's organizational workshop complete with a handout booklet. www.socialthinking.com

Winner, M. (2005) *Think Social! A Social Thinking Curriculum for Teaching School Age Students.* www.socialthinking.com

Winner, M. (2005) *Worksheets! for Teaching Social Thinking and Related Skills.* www.socialthinking.com

Winner, M (2005) **Social Thinking Posters**: Social Behavior Map - Dry Erase Surface, Social Behavior Map for the Classroom, The Boring Moment, Being Part of A Group. Michelle G. Winner, SLP Publisher: San Jose, Ca. (www.socialthinking.com)

Therapeutic Games

- Blurt
- 20 Questions for Kids (1989), University Games.
- Taboo (1989) Milton Bradley Company: MA.
- Guesstures (1990) Milton Bradley Company: MA
- A That's Life Game…What's UP? Ages 11-16, Linguisystems

Some special needs booksellers that are on-line can be accessed at:
www.futurehorizons-autism.com
www.specialneeds.com
www.aspergersyndrome.net

Social Thinking Products by Michelle Garcia Winner

Available from www.socialthinking.com

"Thinking About YOU Thinking About ME" 2nd ed.

Thinking About You Thinking About Me (2nd ed.) is the core book explaining the intervention process that has evolved from the social thinking approach. The second edition of this very popular book was released in August 2007. It incorporates new chapters that update ideas for teaching social information, including explanations of the different levels of perspective taking and how this information relates to providing treatment.

This edition also clearly describes the four steps of communication and related treatment strategies pertaining to practical concepts, such as the ways we maintain communication through physical presence. The expanded assessment section introduces the new "Informal Social Thinking Dynamic Assessment Protocol."

Thinking About YOU Thinking About ME explains why we no longer just teach "social skills" to our brighter students. Instead, we must teach social thinking and related social skills. The book covers content presented in Michelle's workshops, "Nuts & Bolts of Starting Social Thinking Programs" and "Thinking About YOU Thinking About ME."

"Inside Out: What Makes the Person with Social-Cognitive Deficits Tick?"

This book reviews a comprehensive model that helps us understand the social cognitive deficits of persons with diagnosis such as Asperger Syndrome. Through the ILAUGH Model of Social Cognition, parents and educators alike can learn the connection between social thinking and academic skills applied across the school day. By understanding more about abstract/inferential language, perspective taking, and gestalt processing, the reader develops an understanding of how social knowledge not only facilitates social interactions but also helps us to comprehend literature, develop our ideas for written expression, and even impacts our organizational skills. Included are worksheets that can be used in classrooms and in small group settings to help students learn a variety of concepts, including perspective taking. This book covers content presented in Michelle's "Social Thinking Across the Home and School Day" workshop.

"Think Social! A Social Thinking Curriculum for School-Age Students"

This curriculum publication documents how lessons are introduced at Michelle G. Winner's Center for Social Thinking clinic. It demonstrates how to develop a social thinking vocabulary with which to teach children, parents and teachers across the years. It starts with lessons on 'Being Part of a Group' and continues into self-monitoring behavior, the development of language-specific skills, awareness of language meaning, and the development of imagination and wonder towards play/conversation. It introduces ways to explore complex issues of problem solving, hidden curriculum, and social rules as they change during our lifetimes. Eight sections incorporate more than 100 detailed lessons that can span years of treatment.

"WORKSHEETS! for Teaching Social Thinking and Related Skills"

The *Worksheets!* book breaks down abstract social thinking concepts into concrete lessons for students to work on in individual sessions or as part of a larger group. These two hundred worksheets are organized into categories that include friendship, perspective taking, self-monitoring, being part of a group, effective communication, making plans to be with others, problem solving and more. Use these worksheets at school and at home. Many of these lessons are helpful for all students, not just those with obvious social challenges.

"Sticker Strategies to Encourage Social Thinking and Organization"

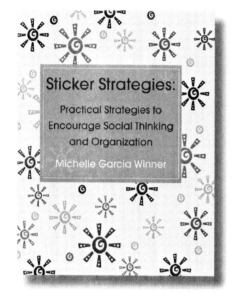

Sticker Strategies includes more than 80 fundamental teaching concepts/student strategies, all printed on color-coded 4x6-inch stickers for application onto a spiral-bound set of index cards. Students use the cards and stickers at their desks while at school or home. This tool allows teachers to help students determine which strategies or social thinking reminders work best for them; a small book of strategies is then developed based on the individual student's needs that the student can transport around campus.

This new product helps students, parents and teachers work towards having students "own their own strategies." The color-coded Strategy Stickers help students learn to be better social thinkers and organize themselves in home and school environments. Blank stickers allow for the creation of individual, customized stickers. Use this book as a launching pad to create your own strategies!

"Social Behavior Mapping: Connecting Behavior, Emotions and Consequences Across the Day"

One of the most successful tools used at Michelle G. Winner's Center for Social Thinking is the Social Behavior Map (SBM). Michelle developed the SBM as a cognitive behavior strategy to teach individuals about the specific relationship between behaviors, other's perspective, other's actions (consequences), and the student's own emotions about those around him or her. The SBM is a visual tool that displays these abstract concepts through a flow chart.

Now, Michelle and her team of talented therapists have created a collection of more than 50 Social Behavior Maps covering a range of topics for home, community and the classroom. *Social Behavior Mapping - Connecting Behavior, Emotions and Consequences Across the Day* is geared for use by parents and professionals to help those with social thinking challenges understand what behaviors are expected and unexpected in a way that makes sense to their way of thinking.

DVD: "Growing Up Social"

Active social skill development begins with birth and expands across our lifetime.

This DVD provides a fascinating look at at how *social thinking* supports the development of social skills from the first year of life, influencing language development and academic success, as well as skills for adult living. Social thinking concepts and strategies will be introduced to support this teaching across the home and school day, including an exploration of how we organize our communicative interactions and utilize active perspective-taking throughout each day. Humor and story telling are used to explore these concepts.

Approximate Running Time: 2 disks at 60 minutes each

DVD: Social Behavior Mapping

Cognitive behavioral techniques are those which help a student to learn the thinking behind expected behaviors. Social Stories™ (developed by Carol Gray) are one type of cognitive behavioral technique for teaching students how to cope in a specific context or with specific people. Social Behavior Mapping is another complimentary method, which helps students to understand how our behaviors (expected and unexpected) impact how people feel, which then impacts how they treat us, which impacts how we feel about ourselves.

Social Behavior Maps demonstrate to students how we all impact each other emotionally and behaviorally. This technique is not a panacea, but instead helps to demystify the complexity of social thought and related behaviors. It is being embraced in classrooms all over the United States.

On this short video clip, the evolution of social behavior mapping is explained along with step-by-step instructions on how to use this valuable treatment strategy. This DVD corresponds with a book called Social Behavior Mapping, also by Michelle Garcia Winner.

Also included on this resource: a brief discussion of Michelle Garcia Winner's other books and DVDs and their applicability for a variety of situations and audiences!

DVD/Video: "Social Thinking Across The Home and School Day"

A Michelle Garcia Winner DVD/VIDEO produced by Carol Gray's "The Gray Center." This four-hour presentation consists of:

• A two-hour workshop reviewing the critical aspects of social cognition that impact social and academic skills. Michelle describes the I LAUGH model of Social Cognition.

• A two-hour demonstration of educational lessons in both group and individual sessions with older and younger students showing how to put theory into action.

Use this indispensible video/dvd to educate teachers and parents about Michelle's ILAUGH model of social cognition. Observe Michelle in a clinical setting, engaged in related educational lessons with students!

DVD + Workbook: "Strategies for Organization–
Preparing for Homework and the Real World"

Organizational skills are traditionally broadly defined and broadly taught. For students with challenges in the areas of multi-tasking or executive functioning, homework management can be overwhelming to the point of meltdown!

Using her warm and engaging teaching style, Michelle presents 10 steps for organizing and producing homework, beginning in early elementary school. While the DVD focuses on how to complete daily homework; the skills learned apply throughout our lives and extend to managing chores, jobs, vacation planning, and more.

The DVD is accompanied by an easy-to-use workbook that includes a project planning guide, time estimation tables, action plans, and problem-solving strategies.

POSTERS!
to Stimulate Social Thinking Skills at Home and at School

Experience a life-size "Boring Moment." See what "Being Part of a Group" looks like in the big picture. Use wall-hung "Social Behavior Maps" to guide students through appropriate behavior and responses.

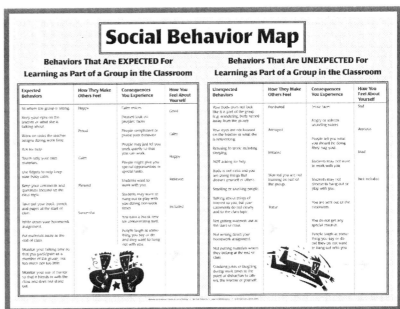

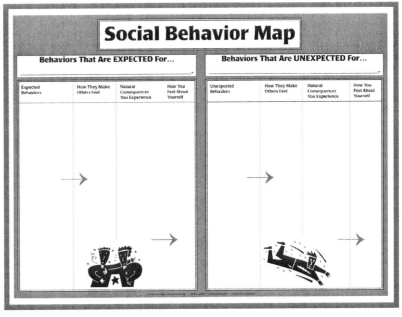

Available from: www.socialthinking.com